Teaching Spiritually Engaged Reading

Edited by David I. Smith, John Shortt,
and John Sullivan

The Stapleford Centre
Nottingham, UK
2007

A Special Issue of
The Journal of Education & Christian Belief
Volume 11:2 (Autumn 2007)

The Stapleford Centre

The Old Lace Mill
Frederick Road,
Stapleford,
Nottingham
NG9 8FN
UK

This themed issue of the Journal of Education and Christian Belief is published in cooperation with the Association of Christian Teachers (Hertfordshire, UK) and the Kuyers Institute for Christian Teaching and Learning (Grand Rapids, MI, USA).

British Library Cataloguing in Publication Data
A catalogue record for this book is available from the British Library.

ISBN: 978-1-902234-65-5
ISSN: 1366-5456

Typeset by Toucan Design, Exeter, Devon, and printed in the USA for the Stapleford Centre by Color House Graphics, Grand Rapids, MI.

JE&CB 11:2 (2007) 1-112   1366-5456

Contents

Editors: David I. Smith, John Shortt, and John Sullivan

Contributors

- **Alan Jacobs** is Professor of English at Wheaton College (Wheaton, Illinois, USA) and author of *A Theology of Reading: The Hermeneutics of Love* (Westview Press, 2001).

- **John Netland** is Professor of English at Calvin College (Grand Rapids, Michigan, USA). His teaching and scholarly interests include English Romantic and Victorian literature, world literature, and the work of the late Japanese novelist Shusaku Endo.

- **Mark Pike** is Senior Lecturer in the School of Education at the University of Leeds (Leeds, UK) and author of *Teaching Secondary English* (Paul Chapman, 2004).

- **C. Rebecca Rine** is a doctoral student in Religious Studies at the University of Virginia (Charlottesville, Virginia, USA). Her focus area, "Scripture, Interpretation, and Practice," involves comparative study of the Abrahamic traditions.

- **Cynthia Slagter** is Associate Professor of Spanish at Calvin College (Grand Rapids, Michigan, USA).

- **David Smith** is Associate Professor of German and Director of the Kuyers Institute for Christian Teaching and Learning at Calvin College. He recently published the volume *Spirituality, Social Justice and Language Learning* (Information Age, 2007).

- **John Sullivan** is Professor of Christian Education at Liverpool Hope University. His special areas of academic interest include Christian higher education, the interconnections between theology, philosophy, and education, and the match between purposes, contexts, and approaches to Christian education. He is currently editing a book on the communication and reception of Christian faith.

JE&CB 11:2 (2007) 5-11   1366-5456

David I. Smith and John Shortt

Introduction: Reading, Spiritual Engagement, and the Shape of Teaching

The various essays included in this volume all rest on two basic premises, both implied in its title. The first is that reading (not just *what* we read, but for present purposes more particularly *how* we read) has something to do with spiritual growth. The second is that the ways in which we teach the art of reading in classrooms across various subject areas have some bearing on how this relationship between reading and spiritual growth takes shape. These two premises invite the conclusion that it is possible to teach with the goal of spiritually engaged reading in mind (and, conversely, that it is possible to teach in ways that make such reading less likely). The essays gathered here work to tease out these basic matters in a more nuanced manner and in both theoretical and practical terms.

Spirituality and Readers

Again, the first premise concerns reading and spiritual growth. The relationships between reading, faith, and spirituality are multiple and complex. There is a long history of Christian concern *that* learners should read – for a faith so bound up with the interpretation of Scripture, the promotion of literacy has commonly been both a by-product of Christian belief and practice and an intentional element of Christian mission and Christian education. Equally longstanding is Christian concern with *what* learners should read – once mastered, reading becomes a core way of sustaining and nurturing faith through the ongoing reading of Scripture and of theological and devotional literature; it also becomes a common way of encountering challenges to that same faith and temptations of varying kinds.

In addition to concern *that* learners read and concern for *what* they read, a third strand in the connection between spirituality and reading – the one foregrounded in this collection of essays – concerns *how* learners read. Believers grow in, clarify, inform, and correct their faith through acts of reading, whether of Scripture or of other texts in which orientation is sought or found, and the qualities that characterize those acts of reading (hurried, reflective, nuanced, careless, self-serving) can both result from and contribute to the shape of a person's faith. Here again, complexities and possibilities multiply; there is a massive literature attempting to define or explain responsible practices of interpretation, or to elucidate the underlying nature of textual encounter. There are books offering guidance, Christian or otherwise, on how to read books intelligently – how to analyze arguments, locate key ideas, and reflect critically on underlying assumptions (e.g., Adler, 1972;

Sire, 1978). The particular focus in the present volume, however, is on the area of overlap or intersection between the "how" of reading in educational settings and the "how" of Christian living: How do the ways in which we teach and learn textual encounter both flow from and contribute to lived faith?

This intersection becomes apparent when one reflects on some of the ways in which the act of reading can vary. Reading is not simply reading – it is practiced differently in different times and places as well as by different individuals (Boyarin, 1992). That reading is more than decoding is obvious as soon as we begin to consider some of the ways in which texts may be read. A text may be read in a cursory or a thorough manner. It may be skimmed and scanned or meditated upon, digested, and obeyed. It may be read once only or returned to for repeated readings. It may be studied sequentially, browsed haphazardly, or used selectively as a reference. It may be read silently or aloud, individually or communally, privately or publicly, for the sake of the reading experience itself or as preparation for a further task, with or without deliberate effort to retain what is read (or to decide what should be retained). Reading may be attentive or inattentive, may do justice or injustice to the text and/or its author, and may be guided into fruitful paths or thrown way off course by a world of prior assumptions, experiences, frames of reference, intentions, and affective states. A reader may approach a text in a manner that displays humility, charity, patience, and submission to its presumed wisdom, or in a manner that displays scorn, haste, or the intent to proudly tear down.

This brief catalog of ways of reading already implies possible intersections between the practice of reading and the practice of the life of faith, intersections that go not only beyond reading as decoding, but also beyond the kinds of tips for reading critically and methodically that form the bulk of how-to-study manuals. The above list illustrates how easily descriptions of how to read well can slip from technique language into virtue language. Qualities such as humility, charity, patience, and justice are goals of Christian maturation, basic ways of approaching the world whose scope and validity extend to how we approach the written words of others (Schwehn, 1993; Jacobs, 2001). Encounter with texts can therefore be a place where such virtues are practiced, and perhaps also where they can be developed. Reading itself can be a form of spiritual discipline, as reflected above in references to meditation, submission, and obedience (Griffiths, 2002).

Encounter with texts can also be a place where the lack of and need for such virtues are brought into the open. When (as happened recently in one of our classes) a student who is achieving a modest grade in a German literature course reads an anthologized poem by Hans Magnus Enzensberger, widely regarded as Germany's most important living poet and one of its most important living intellectuals, and responds in a journal entry with the comment "this poem is pretty sophomoric," it seems plausible to suspect that the problem is more with the character of the student than with the profundity of the poem. Perhaps a little more humility would not be out of place.

Talk of reading silently or aloud, privately or publicly, points to a further dimension of reading as a practice calling upon spiritual and moral resources – as we read, we may enter into relationships not only with the author and the creatures represented in his or her words, but also with other readers and their readings of the text that we have in front of us. We become listeners, co-interpreters, dialogue partners, objectors, judges, encouragers, mockers. Such relationships stretch further our capacities for humility, charity, and justice. Reading is thus not merely an ancillary skill to be first mastered and then pressed into the service of faith-inflected learning; it is itself a practice in which the presence or absence of the fruits of the Spirit may be clearly manifest.

Spirituality and Teachers of Reading

This set of connections, all too briefly sketched here but explored in a more fine-grained manner in the chapters that follow, raises the question implicit in our second basic premise: What bearing does teaching have on all of this? Can we teach in a way that both models Christian forms of engagement with texts and fosters the growth of these in students? How would we go about teaching students not only to read systematically and critically (often enough of a challenge in itself) but also to practice charity, humility, and justice as readers, and to approach texts in a spiritually engaged manner?

To approach such questions may require in the first place an expansion of everyday assumptions about what it means to teach students to read, and about the ways in which such teaching happens in courses that do not have the teaching of reading as their overt agenda. One book on the art of reading opens with the following representative anecdote:

> A few months ago I happened to be present at a dinner where a chance question led to an interesting talk. Some phase of primary education was under discussion; and in the course of it the host, turning to one of the guests, asked, "When did you learn to read?"
> "At three," was the prompt reply, given with a touch of pride.
> "And you?" said the host to the next guest.
> "Oh, I don't know. About five I suppose."
> "And you?" to a lady beyond.
> There was a moment's embarrassed hesitation. And then, with something about scarlet fever, came the confession that she had not learned her letters till she was nine. (Kerfoot, 1916, p. 1)

We tend to associate the idea of "learning to read" with early childhood and with the gradual mastery of the skills of decoding and interpreting text, and the association is strong enough to make the admission that one did not learn to read until the ripe old age of nine embarrassing. When learning to read is thus thought of primarily in terms of learning to decode, the connection with faith easily becomes framed primarily in terms of learning to decode faith-related texts, and the connection with teaching amounts to providing such texts in the classroom. The assumption sometimes appears to be that if the text in use is Christian, or better yet directly biblical, then something edifying must be going on regardless of the kinds of reading activity applied – one thus finds, for instance, learning tasks that have students underlining examples of nouns in a Gospel passage or diagramming sentences from the King James translation of the book of Joshua (Ebner, 1998). While such examples may be extreme in their disjunction between text and task, they differ mainly in degree from more widespread educational instances of classrooms where students are asked to read religiously significant material but the process of reading itself is taken for granted as an unproblematic tool to be applied without significant variation to the texts at hand.

Thinking of, say, college students as still engaged in learning to read does not come naturally; we usually take it for granted that such students already can read, and proceed to assign at least as much reading as can reasonably be expected to fit into the time between classes. Course syllabi and assignment lists routinely detail all manner of things that are to be read but far less commonly specify the manner in which they will be read. Rarely do we inquire into the precise contours of the acts of reading engaged in by students, or make intentional efforts (except sometimes remedially) to shape reading practices. As a result, a great deal of the reading that takes place (perhaps especially, but not only, in higher education) is characterized by students reading at high speed in order to cover the ground in the midst of the obligations of multiple classes; reading superficially, with the aim of avoiding embarrassment in class; reading each work, however complex, once only and accepting that to be a sufficient basis for offering informed opinions about it in class; in sum, reading as hurried consumers of text. If the goal is spiritual growth, then these do not seem the most promising means. If we do not find them particularly promising, the first thing we need to examine is the ways in which teacher behaviors – the ways in which reading activities are framed and structured – are influencing student reading practices.

To be sure, teacher choices are not the sole determinant of students' identities as readers, but they remain centrally important for two reasons. First, it is usually the teacher who determines how reading is practiced in the classroom – what reading practices are modeled to students, whether texts are read aloud or silently, together or alone, sympathetically or critically, once or repeatedly, swiftly or patiently, attentively or at all. Whether intentionally or by default, the teacher leads the shaping of classroom reading practices over time. Second, the particular learning tasks assigned by the teacher, from individual questions assigned in a comprehension exercise to more complex pedagogical activities designed to mediate students' engagement with a text, imply and foster particular reading stances both in and out of class. In a famous example, reader response theorist Louise Rosenblatt (1980) probed the stances toward a poem that were fostered by the accompanying classroom question, What facts does this poem teach you? The student trying to answer this question, even if doing homework alone, away from the classroom's direct influence, is invited into a stance focused on transfer of factual information, and has been made less likely to meditate, for instance, on the personal import of a particular metaphor. This combination of direct power over the shape of shared reading acts and indirect power over a wider range of reading acts through the design of pedagogical tasks places the teacher in the position of significantly influencing the kinds of reading practiced by students. If reading practices do indeed intertwine with matters such as justice, humility, and charity, this is a significant responsibility indeed.

What if our specific choices as teachers can positively influence students' reading practices and experiences in ways that make spiritual growth more likely as an outcome? What concrete choices and design decisions should we be making? Each essay in this volume explores some aspect of how our teaching might better foster the spiritual engagement and spiritual growth of our students through the ways in which reading is practiced in our courses and classrooms.

Alan Jacobs's essay, "On Charitable Teaching," is an exploration of what it could mean to teach in the light of Christian love. He takes up two of the themes he introduced in his earlier work on charitable reading: attentiveness and playfulness. Christian love requires us as teachers to be attentive to our students' desires somewhat in the way that landscape architects are attentive to the desires of the daily users of a space and allow these to play a part in their plans for that space. It is not that these desires must always be accommodated, but that they be given deliberate and careful attentiveness. For teachers for whom the course syllabus has the status of laws set in stone, this is asking too much, but Jacobs argues that what a syllabus really consists of is "an amateurish attempt to scribble down what one can remember of the rules of a children's game" (p. 20). This leads him into discussion of the idea of education as play, and he goes on to suggest that we should see it as leisure, as a gift of God, in which teachers become masters of ceremonies rather than taskmasters.

In his essay on religious reading in historical perspective, John Sullivan argues that what we see as "understanding" is often "overstanding" and that reading is approached in a self-centered and consumerist way that extracts data for the purposes of the individual reader. Religious approaches to reading, on the other hand, require that we stand *under* the text and open ourselves out, in the company of others, to a journey that may change us intellectually, morally, and spiritually. Reading for overstanding is the way of the wandering and detached tourist, whereas reading for understanding is that of the committed and purposeful pilgrim. Sullivan draws upon Augustine and some medieval writers to set forth characteristics and effects of this latter, more holistic approach and how it is linked to religious commitment. He concludes his essay with a section on what he terms the "ecology of reading" in which he lists some of the multiple interacting factors that bear upon students' approaches to reading.

In her essay, "Learning to Read with Augustine of Hippo," Rebecca Rine looks in more detail at what she discerns as a "reading motif" in Augustine's *Confessions* and identifies characteristics of faithful reading similar to those listed by Sullivan. As she puts it, such reading is "goal-oriented and is learned through willful pursuit over time, through a process of trial and error, in the company of other readers" (p. 42). She goes on to argue that teaching to read should echo these characteristics – it should be oriented to a goal (that of the greater love of God and neighbor), it should reflect awareness of a lifelong process of both divine activity and human effort involving trial and error with the humble attitude this requires of teachers and learners, and it should occur within a learning community in which teachers and students learn together.

Trial and error feature prominently in "Misreading Through the Eyes of Faith," David Smith's study of the pedagogical implications of the ways in which Christian students read and misread texts in classrooms. He outlines four models of Christian reading: allegorical reading, in which texts are appropriated as illustrations of Christian theology; perspectival reading, in which the meaning of texts is weighed against the backdrop of Christian convictions; charitable reading, which approaches a text as a neighbor whom we are called to love (a model for which Jacobs argues in his essay); and responsive reading, in which the emphasis is "not only upon the love enacted in attentiveness to the text, but on the degree to which responsiveness to the call heard through the text results in living the life of love" (p. 60). When Smith reflected upon classroom instances of the misreading of texts, he found that they could not always be simply dismissed as errors or simply accepted as valid responses because they evidenced elements of some of these models. He proposes that they be seen instead as being analogous to the interlanguage that occurs in the learning of a second language, and he calls for a pedagogical stance of attentiveness that sees them "as evidence of underlying interpretive approaches that could be nudged toward more mature forms" (p. 62).

In his essay "Who Is My Neighbor?" John Netland writes from out of his classroom experience of teaching world literature and proposes that a hermeneutic of difference be replaced with a hermeneutic of love. Instead of allowing ourselves to be irreducibly defined by those things which make us different from one another, we should see ourselves and others as having "multiple identities as both citizens of the cosmos and residents of particularized, local communities" (p. 71). This enables us as we read world literature to go beyond literary tourism and non-judgmentalism to a reconciling love that frees us from privileging either ourselves or self-discovery to regard ourselves and others, our cultures and theirs, as those we respect enough to question. This, he says, is "an indispensable part of loving our neighbor as ourselves" (p. 76).

The focus shifts from the college classrooms that are in view in other essays in this volume to the teaching of younger children in Mark Pike's essay, "Transactional Reading and Spiritual Investment." Pike addresses homes and schools where parents and teachers seek to teach children to read "wisely and well as citizens of God's kingdom and an increasingly secular society" (p. 83). He suggests that focusing on reading as a transaction between reader and text rather than on the morality of texts or the maturity of readers can provide a biblical approach for Christian educators seeking to invest reading experiences with Christian faith. He also argues that reading is one of the ways Christians should invest in a secular society, and concludes that when readers sow their faith and invest their spiritual lives in their reading transactions, they will reap spiritual growth.

The final essay, "Approaching Interpretive Virtues Through Reading Aloud," is by Cynthia Slagter. She begins by recounting an unforgettable experience she had as an eighth-grader when her class teacher read a story aloud, and she goes on to discuss the place of reading aloud in learning to read more charitably and justly. She advocates the use of carefully structured read-aloud assignments in the classroom as providing for the possibility of a "slower, more intimate connection" (p. 105) between reader and text. New avenues of exploration and interpretation of text are opened "by encouraging multiple readings of a passage, thereby increasing the possibility of understanding and discerning the author's message"

(p. 105). Nuances, inferences, and previously hidden ideas and undertones can come through as, in reading the text aloud, the reader owns it for a time.

We invite readers of this volume to explore these essays attentively, charitably, and humbly, in hope that they might shed at least some light on the possibilities and pitfalls involved in teaching spiritually engaged reading.

Bibliography

Adler, M. J., & Van Doren, C. (1972). *How to read a book* (Rev. ed.). New York: Simon and Schuster.

Boyarin, J. (1992). *The ethnography of reading*. Berkeley and Los Angeles: University of California Press.

Kerfoot, J. B. (1916). *How to read*. Boston and New York: Houghton Mifflin.

Ebner, L. M. (1998). *Learning English with the Bible. Textbook: A systematic approach to Bible-based English grammar*. Chattanooga, TN: AMG Publishers.

Griffiths, P. (2002). Reading as a spiritual discipline. In G. Jones & S. Paulsell (Eds.), *The scope of our art: The vocation of the theological teacher* (pp. 32-47). Grand Rapids, MI: Eerdmans.

Jacobs, A. (2001). *A theology of reading: The hermeneutics of love*. Boulder, CO: Westview Press.

Rosenblatt, L. M. (1980). "What facts does this poem teach you?" *Language Arts, 57*(4), 386-394.

Schwehn, M. (1993). *Exiles from Eden: Religion and the academic vocation in America*. New York: Oxford University Press.

Sire, J. W. (1978). *How to read slowly: A Christian guide to reading with the mind*. Downers Grove, IL: InterVarsity Press.

JE&CB 11:2 (2007) 13-24   1366-5456

Alan Jacobs

On Charitable Teaching

IN EARLIER WORK on the hermeneutics of charity, the author explored the relevance of Augustine's insistence on charity in reading Scripture for interpreters of non-biblical texts. This article shows how one might bring such charitable reading into the classroom and reframe the teacher's task in its light. The article discusses some implications for our understanding of teaching "methods," close attention to students, the nature of syllabi, and the role of attentive playfulness in learning.

A few years ago, I wrote a book called *A Theology of Reading: The Hermeneutics of Love* (Jacobs, 2001). And since what I want to discuss in the current essay – charity in teaching – is for me a kind of outgrowth of that earlier project, I want to begin by offering an overview of my argument in that book. I especially want to discuss how I came to write it, because that's very relevant to the ways in which what I learned from writing that book can be extended into other aspects of the academic life.

About a decade ago now, in preparing for a session of a course I regularly teach in the history of literary criticism, I was rereading Augustine's *On Christian Doctrine*, which is obviously one of the seminal documents in that history. I came across a passage from Book I that was very familiar to me. Here it is:

> Whoever, therefore, thinks that he understands the divine Scriptures or any part of them in such a way that [his interpretation] does not build the double love of God and of our neighbor does not understand [the Scriptures] at all. Whoever finds a lesson there useful to the building of charity, even though he has not said what the author may be shown to have intended in that place, has not been deceived, nor is he lying in any way. (Augustine, 1958, p. 30)

Augustine's insistence on charity as the vital center of biblical interpretation typically leads me into one of my favorite rhetorical set pieces, in which I decry the professionalization of biblical scholarship, its unfortunate absorption into an academic context that cares nothing for the health of the Church and operates on thoroughly uncharitable principles. (I prefer not to think that in so declaiming I could be interpreting the work of biblical scholars in an uncharitable way.)

However, on this particular occasion something rather different occurred to me: that Jesus' insistence on the "law of love" is not relevant only to interpreters of Scripture. If, as Augustine contends, a commitment to double charity – the love of God and the love of one's neighbor – must govern the interpretation of Scripture, it must also govern the interpretation of literature. The fourteenth-century English theologian Richard Rolle, writing on "the law of love," says: "That you may love [Jesus Christ] truly, understand that his love is proved in three areas of your life – in your thinking, in your talking, and in your manner of working" (Rolle, 1988, p. 159). For one whose vocation is to profess literature, the interpretation of non-biblical texts is central to all of these: it is what I think about, it is what I talk about, it is itself my "manner of working." How (I found myself asking) might I interpret the texts I teach charitably?

I set out to write a book not because I knew the answer to that question, but precisely because I did not know, and I now felt obliged to find out – or at least to make some progress toward a better understanding of what, in light of Augustine's comment, I now understood the very core of my vocation to be. Even now I am not sure how much progress I have made: the whole thing seems to me now more than a lifetime's task. But for what it's worth, here are some of the conclusions I have come to:

1. *Love is productive of knowledge.* There are certain circumstances in which the ideal of "detached" or "objective" inquiry is legitimate, but in general only those who care deeply about something can truly know it. There is a lovely passage in Annie Dillard's *Pilgrim at Tinker Creek* in which she describes a visit to a quarter horse ranch in Wyoming owned by her aunt. Annie thinks she can draw, and tries to draw a horse, but when her sheet of drawing paper is passed around the table, it turns out that everyone in that family can draw a horse far better than Annie can. "When the paper came back," she writes, "it looked as though five shining, real quarter horses had been corralled by mistake with a papier-mâché moose; the real horses seemed to gaze at the monster with a steady, puzzled air …. The point is that I just don't know what the lover knows; I just can't see the artificial obvious that those in the know construct. The herpetologist asks the native, 'Are there snakes in that ravine?' 'Nosir.' And the herpetologist comes home with, yessir, three bags full" (Dillard, 1974, pp. 19-20). As Simone Weil insists, the first trait of love is *attentiveness.* More about this later.

2. *Beware of voracity.* Not *veracity* – veracity is a good thing – but *voracity.* Love is attentive, but not all forms of attention are loving. There is a voracious, consuming, stalking kind of attention: a desire to know a person or an object not for love of her, him, or it, but in order to dominate, to exert power, even to consume. This is a dangerous simulacrum of love.

3. *Beware of the Quixotic temptation.* Don Quixote looked around at the world, and where he wished there to be giants rather than mere windmills, there were giants; where he wished there to be armies rather than herds of sheep, there were armies. He loved the world, but he loved it because he had created it in his own image. This is also what Charles Kinbote does to the poetry of John Shade in that great and terrifying book, Nabokov's *Pale Fire* (Nabokov, 1962). I think this is a great temptation for Christian readers of literature – at least it's a pattern that I've often seen repeated over the years: we read books that we want to love, but we wonder whether it is okay to love them if they are not Christian; so we say that they have a "Christian spirit," or if that seems implausible, we say that they are somehow "redemptive." (We do this with movies too.) Some years ago, the great critic

14

and poet William Empson commented acidly on the Christian critics who were claiming that James Joyce is a "great Christian writer" – presumably because his works are so saturated in the Catholic thought in which he was educated. Empson pointed out, and rightly, that it would be more accurate to say that Joyce had a pathological hatred of Christianity.[1] To turn Joyce into a kind of honorary "Christian writer" may seem charitable and even generous, but it indicates a lack of respect for him, a refusal to acknowledge genuine difference.

4. *Practice kenosis.* There is a line of thought in some (especially Eastern) Christian traditions that *kenosis* (the "self-emptying" of the second Person of the Godhead that Paul describes in Philippians 2) requires a complete evacuation of the self. This I do not believe to be correct: as the cultural theorist Mikhail Bakhtin – himself a devout Orthodox believer – argued, when one's self has been wholly evacuated, one can no longer act or respond, but only be the passive receiver of external impressions. But Jesus did act and respond, and God expects us to act and respond, to Him and to one another. As St. Paul puts it, Christ "emptied himself, taking the form of a servant" (Phil 2:7). It is this understanding of *kenosis* that is relevant to the task of charitable reading.[2] One must take the chance of humbling oneself before what one reads, becoming its servant. This is risky, because not every text will reward such humility: but it is only this risk that opens up possibilities for learning from what we read; and it is only a commitment to such humility that can steer us away from a voracious or quixotic falsification of love.

5. *Play.* Much of what we read was written for our enjoyment as well as our edification, and should be received in that spirit. It is neither necessary nor healthy to try to extract every last drop of moral uplift from every last thing we read. Let's have some fun, for heaven's sake. How sad P. G. Wodehouse would be if he learned that people were reading about Bertie Wooster and Jeeves in order to have a better understanding of social class in early twentieth-century England. More about this, too, later.

So there's a potted summary of my argument about charitable reading. But of course my "thinking, talking, and manner of working" do not involve just solitary reading and written scholarship; they also involve teaching. And so I find myself confronted with a problem: Even assuming that what I have learned about charitable reading is valid, how does it translate into the classroom? How do I exemplify it before and with my students? Can I teach them anything about it? These are questions I have been struggling with ever since I started working on my book. I am not sure how much progress I have made, but such as my thoughts are, I offer them now.

My first point is that, on a practical and everyday level, conversations about teaching tend to focus on "styles" and "methods" and tend to be depressingly and repetitively binary. It is always the Liberators versus the Disciplinarians: those who see their task as "empowering" students versus those who insist on the responsibility of teachers to transmit knowledge to the young. It is like an endless game of Point-Counterpoint, with some version of Jane Tompkins eternally at war with some version of Jacques Barzun. So goes the public debate, though if you pick a teacher at random and ask her what side of the debate she is on, she will almost certainly tell you that she occupies intermediate territory: some lecture, some discussion, and some small groups. In fact, teachers often give this answer even when it is not true – that is, even when they really lean heavily to one side rather than the other – and I think that is because we all know it is a rather fruitless debate, and are all secretly dissatisfied with the categories we are offered.

Fortunately for us, this is one of the many situations in academic life where theological thinking comes to the rescue. To consider the task of teaching in the light of Christian doctrine – to ask, "What does my Christian faith teach me about teaching?" – is a sure way to discern the inadequacy of the conventional formulations and to rethink the problems from something close to the ground floor.

Within Christian doctrine, charity – agape, Christian love – is, as Sir Philip Sidney might have put it, *architectonic*. Around it all else is organized; from it all else must flow. Charity, then, must be the virtue for which every Christian teacher (like every other Christian) most consistently and earnestly prays. The famous thirteenth chapter of St. Paul's first letter to the Corinthians could not be clearer on this point. And my insistence here requires me to do something perhaps rather arrogant: to venture to correct, or at least slightly to amend, the emphasis of Nicholas Wolterstorff on "Educating for Shalom" (Wolterstorff, 2004). *Shalom* should indeed be the goal and fulfillment of our educating – as it is the goal and fulfillment of all human history, indeed the eschatological hope of all Creation! – but *shalom* cannot be seriously pursued unless those who pursue it are formed by and in Christian love. This is what St. Paul means when he lists all those virtues that one may have and still be "nothing" if charity is absent. It is through charity and through charity alone that *shalom* can be achieved. *Shalom* is the fully realized communal embodiment of the practice of Christian love.

St. Paul's insistence on the unique indispensability of charity reminds us that it is not enough to pursue *shalom* – it is not even enough to grasp with clarity and insight what *shalom* consists in. One must be a certain kind of person, one must possess a certain character, in order to pursue and understand *shalom* rightly. If we then ask ourselves, what is the form of charity that I require as a teacher? How do I manifest charity in the classroom, or in counseling sessions, or in grading papers? And if we then go on to ask, how must I live, what must I practice, what must I meditate on, in order to achieve this needful charity? – we then discover a whole new set of complexities and difficulties that make the endless debates between the liberators and disciplinarians seem rather trivial, and perhaps altogether beside the point.

Now it is true that some people will immediately say that the teacher who takes her job seriously enough to actually teach (meaning, usually, to lecture) is the teacher who treats her students with real charity; while other people will equally quickly insist that only a decentralized classroom in which students assume full accountability for their own education is truly charitable. And maybe some will say that real charity is practiced by those in the middle, those who take lessons from both camps. We should not listen to any of those people. They are too quick. They *assume*, and such assumption is problematic, not just because it smacks of self-justification but also because we cannot take it for granted that the models of teaching most consistent with Christian charity are already on the table. How radical are the demands of Christian love! The person who loves most deeply lays down her life for her friends; the loving person blesses those who spitefully use him. Is it likely that practices consistent with these demands are built into the already available structures of teaching and learning? No, to seek charity – to seek to become a charitable person – is to open oneself to almost anything. Perhaps everything we think we know is wrong. In the end, nothing may remain of our familiar habits, our favorite strategies. Then again, perhaps all that we do will remain, but renewed, even transfigured. Who can say? If we wish to be open to the mandate of charity, if we are willing to rethink what we habitually do in the classroom in hopes of practicing Christian love toward our students, where do we begin?

I think, first of all, we do *not* begin by learning to throw around the terms *charitable* and *uncharitable*. Too often we call a judgment uncharitable simply because we dislike it and are not able to say why. Every time I have given a talk about my *Theology of Reading* book, someone has stood up at the end and said that because I am critical of Nietzsche, I am therefore uncharitable to him, QED. I finally learned to ask such critics to show me where I have been unfair, unjust, or inaccurate in my interpretations of Nietzsche; then, if such errors are established, we can go on to talk about whether I was also uncharitable. (Not all errors are caused by uncharity.) So even if it strikes you that a student, a colleague, a writer, or a critic is somewhere being uncharitable, it's best not to stop with that impression, but rather to inquire into the possible sources of it. And it is scarcely more helpful to use the term *charitable* as a commendation. Charity is our goal, and uncharity our aversion; but the former is not a treat with which to reward our allies, nor the latter a stick with which to beat our opponents.

So if we do not start there, where do we start? I believe that two of the conclusions I came to in my inquiry into charitable reading may be especially useful to us as we try to consider the task of teaching in the light of Christian love.

The first of these is *attentiveness*. It is extraordinarily difficult to pay true attention either to ourselves or to other people. Attentiveness is the pearl of great price for teachers and students alike. For students who are interested in this topic, I would recommend a remarkable lecture given by Simone Weil to a gathering of girls at one of the secondary schools where she taught in the 1930s. It is called "Reflections on the Right Use of School Studies with a View to the Love of God" (Weil, 1951, pp. 105-116). Weil's key insight is that attentiveness, once achieved, is transferable. If you learn to give sustained and intense attention to a problem in your school work, you will be better positioned to give such attention to your suffering neighbor, and to God in prayer. And because it does not come naturally to us to love God or our neighbor, the subjects we like least in school are the ones that can be most spiritually useful to us, because attentiveness to them will be hard-won and therefore more useful when we turn to other things we would rather not do. "If we concentrate our attention," Weil says, "on trying to solve a problem in geometry, and if at the end of an hour we are no nearer to success than we were at the beginning, we have nevertheless been making progress each minute of that hour in another more mysterious dimension. Without our knowing or feeling it, this apparently barren effort has brought more light into the soul. The result will one day be discovered in prayer" (p. 106). It is vital that we practice such discipline, Weil argues, because "warmth of heart" does not really count for much in prayer, though we would like to think it does. Sudden loving feelings for people will not sustain us for more than a few seconds before they fade, whereas "quality of attention" sustains prayers for far longer.

Of course, Weil's insight is just as relevant to teachers as to students, insofar as teachers are also learners. But it is relevant to teachers in a unique way, because our students are not just our neighbors; they are neighbors who have been placed, for a season and in a limited way, under our care. We have an especially great obligation to be attentive to them. This seems obvious, and I guess it is, but after reading Weil's essay I have a sense that I set my standards for attentiveness very low indeed. But how to build true attentiveness?

In addressing this question I want to borrow a concept from landscape architecture and the sociology of crowd behavior: the concept of "desire lines." When landscape architects lay out a public space where many people walk, if it is not one vast expanse of concrete, but has some grass or flowerbeds, they will construct sidewalks and other pathways to take people from one significant site to another. But as we all know, if those pathways are not laid out in just the way that people want to go, people will ignore the concrete and cut across lawns, eventually wearing the grass into dirt paths. This happens on college campuses more than anywhere else. As we also know, the grass will not be worn randomly, but very distinct paths will emerge very quickly. These are called "desire lines." Landscape architects – or perhaps the authorities who govern such public spaces – have basically two responses to desire lines. One response is to find ways to thwart people from making them – to put up "KEEP OFF THE GRASS" signs and even build barriers. The other response is to acknowledge the desire lines and pave them over so people can use them even more readily. There is even a movement among designers that calls for planting grass over the whole space, waiting to see where the desire lines form, and only then paving the pathways. (As far as I know, the first time this practice was followed was when the campus of the University of California at Irvine was built in the 1960s.)

Until relatively recently, designers and architects either ignored desire lines or were frustrated by them, seeing them as incoherent impositions on the orderly beauty of a design. Once you start paying attention to these lines, they can be seen as themselves a kind of design – *emergent* design, you might say, rather than centrally planned. Some landscape architects now talk about a cooperatively designed environment, in which the preferences of a space's daily users are allowed to play a part.

What I am suggesting is that, if we teachers become more truly attentive to our students, we will notice what their habitual concerns are, what kinds of questions they want to ask, what readings or assignments make them uncomfortable, and so on. If we consider the kinds of papers our students want to write, and often do write – sometimes in opposition to, or at least at a tangent from, the kinds of papers we assign – we can begin to trace their desire lines, the paths they insist on taking in resistance to the officially designed paths. I think charity requires us to cultivate this kind of attention. It does not necessarily require us to *accommodate* those desires, to alter our "official" paths so that they meet student preferences; in fact, often we should not do that. But we have an advantage that landscape architects do not have: not only can we change the pathways, we can move the buildings. That is, we can reconfigure our classes in such a way – by altering curriculum or assignments, yes, but also by providing different contexts, or just better explanations – as to make our official paths the most comfortable ones for the students to follow. We can only make such adjustments, whether rhetorical or substantive, if we are paying close attention, if we are asking questions and listening to the answers. We can make a start just by noting body language and facial expressions, of course; but I know I could do a much, much better job of tracking the patterns of questions and comments, and noting the topics students like to write papers about.

I want to tell a story now about something a former colleague of mine did, because this story both illustrates a way of being attentive and also leads to the second recommendation I want to make. Once, about halfway through a course in African-American literature, he was teaching Toni Morrison's *Beloved*. Because *Beloved* is such an important novel, he had assigned two weeks to it; but at the end of the two weeks, he was very dissatisfied. He felt that his concerns about the book and the questions he wanted to raise had not been of much interest to the students, and he felt that he had been ill-prepared to respond to the questions and concerns that had been most important to them. Only as the time allotted for the book came to an end did he realize that he now knew how to address what the students wanted to know, and also understood how he might have presented to them the issues and themes he thought central to the novel. He even thought he could see ways of linking their thoughts with his own.

Now, if he had merely kept notes on these discoveries and implemented them the next time he taught the class, I would certainly have applauded him for his charitable attentiveness to his students – and asked myself whether, in a similar situation, I would have been observant and sensitive enough to act as wisely. However, he did something different. On the last day assigned to discussion of *Beloved*, he walked into the classroom and said, "You know, this discussion didn't go nearly as well as I would have liked. I didn't teach this book very well, and I did a poor job of answering your questions. And it is a very, very important book. So on Monday, let's start over. Let's go back to the beginning and take two more weeks, and this time we'll make some real progress in understanding this novel. I'll need to make some adjustments in the schedule, and we'll not get around to reading one of the books I assigned, but we just need to get this right, or at least do it better."

I have no idea how the class as a whole reacted, but I know that several students were completely freaked out. Some felt that their trust in their teacher's competence had been undermined; others – the more anal-retentive of the group – were outraged that in mid-semester a syllabus was changed. Apparently they thought of syllabi as documents scarcely more eligible for revision than the tablets Moses brought down from the mountain. At least one, I am especially sorry to say, was angry at having purchased a book that he did not need to buy, and could not get a full refund from the college bookstore.

Now, I am not sure that what my colleague did was the best thing, and I probably would not have done it myself – though whether that is wisdom or cowardice on my part, I do not know. But the intensity of the negative reactions I heard really surprised me, and made me glad that he did what he did, because it revealed to me certain odd expectations teachers and students alike have about that strange thing, the course syllabus.

Some decades after the publication of *The Waste Land*, T. S. Eliot gave a lecture in which he described the circumstances of its publication and especially the decision to add the later-to-be-famous Notes to the end of the poem: just before publication, "it was discovered that the poem was inconveniently short, so I set to work to expand the notes, in order to provide a few more pages of printed matter, with the result that they became the remarkable [exhibition] of bogus scholarship that is still on view today" (Eliot, 1957, p. 121).[3] In my view, that is what almost every course syllabus is: a remarkable exhibition of bogus scholarship. A syllabus, by its very nature, is a sham. It gives the appearance of formidable erudition, organized and deployed in a form so rational, so methodologically rigorous, that Thomas Aquinas, were he to see it, might well weep with envious admiration.

In point of fact, and in contrast, what a syllabus *really* consists of is an amateurish attempt to scribble down what one can remember of the rules of a children's game. Like the rules of a game, the contents of a syllabus are effectively arbitrary; like any attempt to record such rules, a syllabus always leaves something out – and what it leaves out, at some point in the playing of the game, usually proves to be vital. In *Discipline and Punish* Foucault writes that "the examination" – by which he means the medical examination, the classroom examination, and several others – presents itself as "the ceremony of power and the form of the experiment, the deployment of force and the establishment of truth" (Foucault, 1979, p. 192). So too, in a different way, does the syllabus. What my colleague performed – what students and probably some administrators and fellow faculty found so disturbing – was a revelation of the real character of the syllabus, an exposure of its pretense to organize knowledge and establish truth. Behind the curtain, it turns out, is no omnipotent wizard, just a little man who could not frighten a gnat.

In saying "That didn't work very well, let's try it again," my colleague revealed not just that teaching is for the teacher a form of dramatic self-presentation as an expert or true pedagogue – everyone knows that – but rather that education, *paideia*, is in its very organizational structure a game, a kind of play-acting or just playing. It is this idea of education as *play* that connects us again to what I learned in writing my book on charitable reading – and I will confess now that it was not until that book was almost finished that I came to understand the intimate relationship between charity and playfulness. If I could write the book again, that would be its central theme.

In what follows I am going to draw on the work of the great Catholic scholar Josef Pieper, and especially his book *Leisure, the Basis of Culture*. It is Pieper who reminds us that the Greek word for leisure is *skole*, from which we get our word *school*. *School* does not feel very leisurely to students, but with some effort that can be corrected. One can only go to school if one is free from the responsibility to work for a living: after all, the Greek word for work, or one of them, is *ascholia*, "un-leisure." Every college student is able to study because of someone's labor, past (in the case of scholarships), present (in the case of students whose way is paid by parents or themselves), or future (in the case of students who take out loans that they will eventually have to repay). But however it is paid for, the time that we are in school as students is indeed leisure time, and should be treated as such.

This is particular important in schools like Wheaton College, where I teach. In addition to being a Christian college, Wheaton is also a liberal arts college. That description arises in the Middle Ages in the distinction between the *ars servile*, which have defined utilitarian functions, and the *ars liberale*, which are "liberal" in that they are liberated from the need for utilitarian justification, and also in that they provide intellectual liberation for those who study them. We tend to think of vocational training as being "servile" in this particular sense, and believe that the various disciplines that come to mind when we call up the term "liberal arts" are necessarily "free" from such servility. But in fact this is not true. In his *Idea of the University*, Cardinal Newman (1873/1996) points out that if you study theology in order to preach better sermons or write better catechisms, then theology is not for you a "liberal art." Now Newman does not think that theology is lowered by being put to use – far from it: he just wants us to be clear in our terminology. In the same way, I would argue, when I teach an English class with a view toward preparing my students for graduate school, our studies of that material are not truly liberal; instead, they are servile. Again, as Newman (1873/1996, p. 82) indicates, that is not a bad thing; but it is a *different* thing than fully liberal study. And we all know that there are enormous pressures – from students, from their parents, from accreditation agencies, and probably from our own need for self-justification – to make all the liberal arts into servants of something.

In *Leisure, the Basis of Culture* Pieper is very aware of these pressures. Even though they may have been far less strong when he wrote the book in 1947 than they are in our time and place, we know he is part of our world when he encourages us to ask this question: "Is there a sphere of human activity, one might even say of human existence, that does not need to be justified by inclusion in a five-year plan and its technical organization? Is there such a thing, or not?" (Pieper, 1947/1963, p. 34). Pieper understands that while we may nominally believe in such a sphere, it is enormously difficult for teachers to act as though we believe in it and reside within it.

Pieper's argument in response to this situation is subtle, but ultimately compelling, and of particular relevance for anyone who teaches at a Christian institution. He believes that one can only think of education as leisure if one thinks of it as a gift. But a gift from whom? From God, of course. And therefore leisure, he claims, must be linked to, and even derived from, the worship of God. "Culture depends for its very existence on leisure," he argues, "and leisure, in its turn, is not possible unless it has a durable and consequently living link with the *cultus*, with divine worship" (p. 17).

If this is right, then Christian teachers at Christian institutions are uniquely situated to cultivate a leisurely model of education, and thereby to strengthen culture itself. As Christians who already participate in the worship of God, we ought especially to think of our time together in "school" as a gift: the gift of leisure, of "free" time from work for students, and for teachers the wonderful opportunity to be not so much taskmasters as masters of ceremonies. Indeed, given Pieper's emphasis on the vital role of festivity in the life of leisure – he does not think that leisure can be sustained without periodic pauses for deeply ceremonial festivals of celebration – perhaps we should sometimes think of ourselves as Lords of Misrule, as people devoted to turning the practices of everyday life upside down. After all, one of the ways of "preparing young people for the real world" – preparing them morally and spiritually, that is – is to remind them that the "real world" could be other, that its habitual practices are not graven in the stone of reality, but rather have arisen from social convention and convenience. This is what, in medieval culture, the Lords of Misrule did: not permanently overthrow the Powers That Be, but for a season displace them, thereby revealing that all who hold authority do so at the discretion of a God who could, if He chose, shape the world in quite another mold. If God is sovereign, all human social structures are contingent: this is the constant lesson of the Lords of Misrule.[4]

In saying that we should be masters of ceremonies rather than taskmasters, I am not arguing that we "lower our academic standards," or cease to take the labor of instruction and assessment seriously: my argument actually has nothing to do with such matters. I am speaking of the life-context in which we conduct our work, the frame of thanksgiving, and indeed even celebration within which assignments and assessments take place. We should take our work seriously in just the same way that we should take a game seriously, playing to win but always subliminally aware that it is but a game, that its rules are for our pleasure and convenience. That is what my former colleague was doing when he gave himself a "do-over" on Morrison's *Beloved*. You can tell a playful educator less by the grades she hands out than by the spirit in which she gives them; and you can tell a *successfully* playful educator by the spirit in which her students receive those grades.

As I make this comparison – between our organization of our academic work and the playing of games – I believe the comparison is vital, but not as effective as it should be, because Americans have managed to turn almost every game available to us into yet another kind of work. Blame for this can be laid at any number of feet, but I especially lament the rise of professional sports around the world in the past century. This has had, I believe, a devastating effect on our capacity for leisure. The sports we see daily on television and read about in our papers are not play, but labor, but they are the models many of us have in mind when we teach our children to play games. As a result, for many children, especially American children, sports are often less leisurely than anything else in their lives.

All the more reason, then, to consider it an act of charity – of Christian love – not just to accept, but to announce and heighten the playful, game-like character of education. This is not to deny, or even to minimize, a commitment by educators to be engaged in the work of forming persons with certain characters

– and, for Christian teachers, to be about the work of "schooling Christians," as Stanley Hauerwas (1992) puts it. But one of the ways we can love our neighbors when we teach is to remind them, and to remind ourselves, that education is a gift of leisure, and that the ways we structure that leisure are, if not utterly arbitrary, at least potentially playful. We exhibit charity towards our neighbors, towards God, and even towards ourselves when we achieve a humorous realization of our own limitations. The poet W. H. Auden (1962, p. 145) offers a wise word when he tells us that in this fallen world the voice of agape can only speak in a comic voice.

Attentive playfulness is, then, what I am counseling – to myself no less than to my readers. To that some might say, that's it? Pay attention, have fun? These are his recommendations? But the real problem with my recommendations is not that they are obvious or trivial; it is that they are nearly unimaginable. I do not know how to pay attention. I feel hopeless at the thought of trying to resist the truly deadly seriousness with which modern American education takes itself – the eternally somber pretense of purely technical competence, or therapeutic mastery, which of course just makes students, parents, and politicians mock or sneer at educators. However, I think Christian charity demands these things of me – and I should not be surprised: after all, does not Christ always ask me to do what I know I cannot achieve and perhaps cannot even imagine? In what I am asked – or what at least I feel I am asked – there lies the possibility to reconceive my daily work as a teacher in ways that could be almost infinitely rewarding.

Notes

1   "A strong drive has been going on to recover the children for orthodox or traditional religious beliefs; … and when you understand all that, you may just be able to understand how they manage to present James Joyce as a man devoted to the God who was satisfied by the crucifixion. The concordat was reached over his dead body." (Empson, 1984, p. 216).

2   Bakhtin writes about this matter in his early (1929) work *Toward a Philosophy of the Act* (Bakhtin, 1993). I make this argument in far more detail in my essay "Bakhtin and the Hermeneutics of Love" (Jacobs, 2001).

3   Eliot actually writes "exposition" rather than "exhibition," but the latter surely was what he meant to write.

4   One of the best overviews of the Lord of Misrule tradition remains C. L. Barber's *Shakespeare's Festive Comedy* (Barber, 1959), especially chapters 1-3.

Bibliography

Augustine. (1958). *On Christian doctrine* (D. W. Robertson, Trans.). Indianapolis: Bobbs-Merrill.

Bakhtin, M. M. (1993). *Toward a philosophy of the act* (V. Liapunov, Trans.). Austin, TX: University of Texas Press.

Barber, C. L. (1959). *Shakespeare's festive comedy: A study of dramatic form and its relation to social custom*. Princeton, NJ: Princeton University Press.

Dillard, A. (1974). *Pilgrim at Tinker Creek*. New York: Bantam.

Eliot, T. S. (1957). The frontiers of criticism. In Eliot, T.S. *On poetry and poets*. New York:

Farrar.

Empson, W. (1984). Ulysses: Joyce's intentions. In W. Empson (Ed.), *Using Biography*. Cambridge: Harvard University Press.

Foucault, M. (1979). *Discipline and punish: The birth of the prison*. New York: Vintage Books.

Jacobs, A. (2001). *A theology of reading: The hermeneutics of love*. Boulder, CO/New York: Westview Press.

Jacobs, A. (2001). Bakhtin and the hermeneutics of love. In S. M. Felch & P. J. Contino (Eds.), *Bakhtin and religion: A feeling for faith* (pp. 25-45). Evanston, IL: Northwestern University Press.

Hauerwas, S., & Westerhoff, J. H. (Eds.). (1992). *Schooling Christians: "Holy experiments" in American education*. Grand Rapids, MI: Eerdmans.

Morrison, T. (1987). *Beloved: A novel* (1st ed.). New York: Knopf/Random House.

Nabokov, V. V. (1962). *Pale fire: A novel*. London: Weidenfeld and Nicolson.

Newman, J. H. (1996). *The idea of a university*. New Haven, CT/London: Yale University Press. (Original work published 1873)

Pieper, J. (1963). *Leisure, the basis of culture* (A. Dru, Trans.). New York: Mentor. (Original work published 1947)

Rolle, R. The law of love. In D. L. Jeffrey (Ed.), *The law of love: English spirituality in the age of Wyclif* (pp. 155-62). Grand Rapids, MI: Eerdmans, 1988.

Weil, S. (1951). *Waiting on God*. London: Routledge & K. Paul.

Wolterstorff, N. (2004). *Educating for shalom: Essays on Christian higher education*. Grand Rapids, MI: Eerdmans.

JE&CB 11:2 (2007) 25-38   1366-5456

John Sullivan
Understanding and Overstanding: Religious Reading in Historical Perspective

I SUGGEST THAT, in universities, we often use the word 'understanding' when we mean 'overstanding'. This is connected to relying on limited approaches to reading, ones that are forgetful of religious ways of reading. I offer a critical retrieval of religious ways of reading, practised in the past, and suggest how they might be included in the university today, thereby providing a richer form of educational experience for students.

I want to suggest that we often use the word 'understanding' when we mean 'overstanding', and that this usage is linked to a range of approaches to reading in academic contexts, specifically a forgetting of assumptions and habits that were once integral to the reading practices sponsored and modelled by religious believers. It is only too easy to forget, as English scholar Alan Purves has argued, how central religious reading once was to the practice of reading in general. Purves (1998, p. 62) claims that "it is in religious contexts that reading has been practiced by a large part of the population over the years. Church reading was the first introduction to reading for countless generations, and for many it is so still." What I wish to bring out in this paper is how religious approaches to reading differ, sometimes starkly, from the ways we usually read, and encourage others to read, especially the ways we do so as a central activity of the university. Insofar as schoolteachers internalise and become wedded to contemporary approaches to and assumptions about reading from their academic and professional formation at university, they are likely to promote these in their work in schools throughout their career. My focus here will not be on reading in elementary and secondary schools, but in universities. However, I believe that the contrast we encounter when we consider some previous modes of reading should at least give Christian teachers at all levels of education pause for thought. In each of these work contexts they might even judge that, in some circumstances, they can alert students to the possibility of alternative ways to approach their reading.

In section one I indicate a more expansive appreciation than is common of what reading can do for readers. Then, in section two I draw upon Augustine and some medieval writers to illustrate this more expansive approach to reading, its links with religious commitment, and its promotion of understanding. Finally, in section three I show how this contrasts with the attitudes built into more recent approaches to understanding, which I characterise as being better described as overstanding. I end with a very modest way of starting to get students to reflect on the multiple factors that bear upon our reading.

Let me clarify the specific focus and therefore also expose some of the limitations of this paper. My intention is not to survey the theoretical literature about reading. This would have required attention to such writers as Cavallo & Chartier (2003) on the history of reading; or Jauss' reception aesthetics and literary hermeneutics (Rush, 1997); or Kivy's (2006) work on the performance of reading; and the seminal work of Rosenblatt (1978) on transactional theories of reading. Rather, I seek to retrieve insights about reading drawn from some earlier theological and spiritual traditions, suggesting that these insights have applicability beyond their original settings and beyond the reading of religious texts. By contrasting a more full-blooded or holistic approach to reading, one that engages the reader more comprehensively and that makes greater demands on him or her, I hope to show the limitations of a consumerist and instrumental approach to reading that encourages students to interrogate a text for useful data they can deploy without being changed in the process. In my view, modes of reading other than the ones I draw attention to here are both legitimate and necessary for university students, and I continue to encourage their use. I do not hope or expect that all reading should display features of the more expanded interpretation of reading evident in the past; I am only advocating that some reading should do so. My focus is not on techniques of reading but on the continuing relevance of some past assumptions about its purpose and the activities and attitudes that surround and constitute it. My argument is that students – in engaging with some theological, spiritual and religious texts, and also as they read historical, political and literary texts – would benefit from receiving an opportunity to add to their repertoire of ways of reading the kinds of reading described here. By itself, the more religious form of reading described here would be insufficient for a contemporary university's academic requirements in any particular discipline, including theology. However, in my view, failing to give students an opportunity to experience what this kind of reading offers and demands would sell them short and impoverish their appreciation of the range of reading open to them.

I make four assumptions for this paper. Two are taken from Mark Pike and two from Chris Anderson. From Pike I accept the view that "Reading is an essentially 'religious' activity, not in the sense that it is related to an established religion, but because it is value-laden and cannot be separated from the beliefs and values of readers and writers" (Pike, 2006, p. 284). I also take from Pike the judgement that "reader response theory ... has demonstrated that what a person believes influences how they read (as well as what they read and why they read)" (Pike, 2006, p. 284; see also Smith, 2004, on aesthetic reading, spiritual development and challenging readers to change their lives). I will argue that we would do well to acknowledge the force of these two points and apply them in teaching students how to read more deeply, self-reflectively and fruitfully. I concur with Chris Anderson that "all teachers at the university are teachers of reading" and that "reading requires community" (Anderson, 2004, p. 71). With regard to his first point, the universality of the task of teaching reading, I hope that, although my own teaching is based in a theology department, key aspects of eliciting better reading in that context have application in other disciplines. His second point, the role of community in creating the conditions for adequate reading, will be developed here only indirectly, and in two different respects. First, I argue that we should challenge students to move away from an individualist and consumerist approach to reading, where they seek to extract data for their own purposes, and move them closer to ways of reading that require of them a degree of adjustment to and indeed submission (at least provisionally) to the journey expected by the text. Such "opening out" of the student is likely to be more conducive of community in that it breaks down some elements in our self-centredness. Second, I give due attention, in the last part of the paper, to the ecology of reading, the multiplicity of factors at work in influencing reading and their mutual interaction in classroom settings.

1. Reading as a journey which changes us

I do not think many students expect their reading to change them or even to make demands on them. They look at it as an act of consumption, where they seek something which gives them the building blocks to address some assignment, which is itself a necessary hurdle along the way to accumulating a qualification. The act of reading is for a very limited purpose; once found and deployed, the information gathered can be jettisoned, having passed through the readers but without having changed them in any substantial way. The assumption is that the item of text being read is equally accessible to any reader of similar intelligence, regardless of that reader's basic convictions, character, lifestyle or the company they keep. These elements in their life are considered private matters and quite irrelevant to what they can gain from their reading. It is not the business of the teacher to suggest a connection between these aspects of their life and what understanding is made possible via reading.

An alternative view considers reading an exercise in change, part of a personal journey which could be described as a pilgrimage, or as an ascent. It is not just like scanning a map; it goes beyond a passive observation of the words and thoughts of another. Serious reading prompts us to reach up to the thought of another, to clamber onto the path they offer us, to cross a threshold, to enter into an idea, a tradition, a form of conduct or a way of life. This more expansive appreciation of reading combines inwardness, commitment and openness to transcendence. It engages the personal life of readers. It presses them to decide, to judge and in light of this to give themselves, to adhere to a concept, a skill, a virtue, a practice. In doing so, it reveals illusions which are to be left behind, it exposes bad practices which are to be given up and it paves the way to a receptive openness to change.

Let me suggest several phrases that religious readers in the past would have associated with the notion of reading: to remember rightly, to perceive accurately, to believe reliably, to respond promptly, to relate responsibly, to interpret justly, to love appropriately, to belong generously, to share joyfully, to surrender willingly, to pray fervently. At first sight, these phrases can strike us as having little to do with reading per se, decoding a text or finding information, for example. They appear to import all kinds of extraneous, unnecessary and, indeed, intrusive expectations. They link reading with habit, repetition and memory, with discipline and obedience, with conversion and transformation, with community and indwelling, with self-scrutiny, docility, humility and character, and with worship. This more full-blooded set of associations with the act of reading, though not restricted to Christians, is certainly very much in harmony with, even integral to, their tradition. This mentality is indirectly echoed, for example, in such biblical phrases as "But the wisdom that comes from heaven is first of all pure; then peace-loving, considerate, submissive, full of mercy and good fruit, impartial and sincere" (James 3:17 NIV) and "If you hold to my teaching, you are really my disciples. Then you will know the truth, and the truth will set you free" (John 8:31b-32). The height of human wisdom is here a gift from above, rather than achieved through effort, virtuosity or technical expertise or dexterity; it embraces the whole person; it links character and insight; it emerges not through being a rule unto oneself but through being a willing disciple; it is not disconnected from the whole pattern of our choices and desires. Thus, where we read (our location), why we read (our purpose), how we read (the method we use), who we are (our identity and character) and who we are with when we are reading (the company we keep) all interrelate and influence each other.

Paul Griffiths (1999) distinguishes religious from consumerist reading, claiming that academic life encourages the latter, while neglecting the former. Religious reading depends on a certain kind of relationship between the reader and what is read, a relationship that allows the text to address, to question and to challenge the reader, and at the same time it adopts an attitude of reverence and obedience towards the text. Rather than standing in authority over the text, interrogating it with critical tools, deferring commitment, questioning its authenticity, the religious reader stands *under* or in the light of such a text. This kind of understanding entails a willingness to be vulnerable to the message contained in a text, submitting to its power, allowing it time to penetrate one's thinking and feeling, and appreciating its resonance. By trusting its source, inhabiting its ambience and participating in the community which is the proper location for its interpretation, religious readers find themselves able to attain a depth of understanding that cannot be reached by consumerist reading and the detached use of critical methodologies. Religious reading, seen in this light, requires relations between readers and texts that are simultaneously "attitudinal, cognitive, and moral; [such relations] imply an ontology, an epistemology, and an ethic" (Griffiths, 1999, p. 41).

This is a view of reading that makes demands on us, rather than one where we make demands on the object of our reading. Rather than making the text answer our questions and somehow fit into the categories of our understanding, already arrived at in advance of the act of reading, the expectation was that readers entered into a moral relationship with what they read, one where readers are led rather than lead and where readers should conform themselves to the text as they would to the demands of a tutor. Of course, it is legitimate for us to make demands on what we read, but if the demands are always unilateral, from us to the material being read, we will miss too much. We will be trying to stand over what we read, but in achieving such overstanding, we may fail to understand. In the study of religion, for example, this distinction between understanding and overstanding can cast light on such questions as Will we study religion on *our* terms or on *its* terms? Will we look *at* a religion, or will we look *through* it at the world and at life? Would it be a fair analogy to ask, If you cannot climb a mountain without being physically fit, can you attain religious truth without developing spiritual capacities? This is to suggest not that religious truth is the fruit of human effort, but that our capacity to reach any worthwhile appreciation of such truth is obstructed or hindered by lack of spiritual development. The more expansive approach to reading recalled here raises issues for our consideration, our motivations, our intentions, our attitudes, our purposes, our readiness for and our approach to reading.

A religious way of reading does not treat the individual as the basic unit; it gives priority to the religious community. It does not adopt a detached and distant perspective; it expects engagement, participation and commitment. It does not divorce the personal qualities of the seeker from the public methods and outcomes of the search; it expects conversion and transformation of life as the price – and the key – for unlocking the doors to the treasures held within the tradition. Religious accounts of the world are learned in a social, linguistic and institutional context (Griffiths, 1999, p. 13), though this does not mean that there is a deterministic relation between relevant practice and religious accounts. There is an expectation in religious learning that the personal life of the student will be modified, redirected and brought into line with the object of study. The will must be ordered and the appetites harnessed, away from self-centred gratification and towards God and other people (Griffiths, 1999, p. 17). The transformational practices enjoined on us as essential elements in religious reading give us a new identity, one that changes us intellectually as well as morally and spiritually.

Let me give an example of the difference between the understanding and the overstanding mentality. The religious thinker Friedrich von Hügel once described an experiment required of a prospective student by the Unitarian preacher James Martineau (Von Hügel, 1926, pp. 126-129). The student, already strongly analytical, sharply critical of religion and highly cerebral in his approach to his studies, was asked to spend two periods of six months with very different communities. The first was to be with uncultured, narrow-minded but believing peasants in Westphalia. Then he was to spend six months with highly intelligent and sceptical medical students in Berlin. His reflection on how best to approach the study of religion was to be informed by his experience of how these two vastly different communities coped with their hopes and fears and how they responded to the successes and problems they encountered. The student took the view that the piety of the former, despite all its limitations and prejudices, took them further towards wisdom for a worthy life than the scepticism and freedom of the latter group. For all their shortcomings, the believing peasants acknowledged the givenness and objectivity of religious truth; they knew they stood (whether in darkness or in light) under its authority; they knew they should allow themselves to be conformed to the reality that stood over them, even if their progress was faltering and erratic. On the other hand, the medical students, in their intellectual pride and self-confidence, stood over a religion they cut even further down to the scale and meaning allowed it by their conceptual apparatus and methodology.

2. An earlier way of reading

I once bought a poster which described a medieval allegory of the scribe's tools. The only attribution was to an anonymous medieval monastic sermon from Durham. On the poster the tools of a scribe were each viewed as spiritual aids for a Christian life.

The parchment on which we write is pure conscience.
The knife that scrapes it is the fear of God.
The pumice that smoothes the skin is the discipline of heavenly desire.
The chalk that whitens it signifies an unbroken meditation of holy thoughts.
The ruler is the will of God.
The straight edge is devotion to the holy task.
The quill, its end split in two for writing, is the love of God and of our neighbour.
The ink is humility itself.
The illuminator's colours represent the multiform grace of heavenly wisdom.
The writing desk is tranquillity of heart.
The exemplar from which a copy is made is the life of Christ.
The writing place is contempt of worldly things, lifting us to a desire for heaven.

This allegory nicely illustrates some of the points made above about a more full-blooded set of associations linked with the act of reading and study. It clearly locates the path of learning with the path of discipleship. Augustine of Hippo similarly links the curriculum for study with the pilgrimage towards God. The academic and the spiritual, far from being separate, are closely integrated. John MacInnis shows how, in his *De Doctrina Christiana* (2.7.9-11), Augustine describes the various steps along which a pilgrim reader will travel: from fear to piety, to knowledge, to fortitude, to counsel, to purgation of the eyes of the heart, to single-mindedness, to wisdom. "For Augustine, attitudes of piety and docility are what we might call today preconditions for approaching sacred texts (3.1.1) …. A personal posture of faith, which shows itself in prayer, is indispensable for approaching the inspired word" (MacInnis, 2002, p. 386). In his *Confessions* (10:17-35) Augustine places huge emphasis on the importance of memory within the act of reading. As Brian Stock shows in his magisterial work, *Augustine the Reader*, Augustine unites study, remembering and self-examination (Stock, 1996). One might contrast Augustine's approach to reading with contemporary surfing of the Internet or with forms of reading that resemble tourism. Tourists make short-term visits. They come as outsiders and remain outsiders by the time they leave. Based on their own idiosyncratic and spur-of-the-moment preferences, they pick and choose what to experience in the land they visit. They observe, rather than participate in, the events offered for their entertainment. There is all the difference in the world between aimless wandering and purposeful pilgrimage.

For many medieval readers "reading is an activity … [for] the authorial 'leading by the hand' of the reading soul unto the beatific vision" (Candler, 2006, p. 18). Reading involved the whole person; it was founded on and framed by the activity of worship; it was set in a community context; it was carefully reinforced by diverse sensory cues, including posture and gesture (for the role of gesture in learning to be members of the body of Christ, see Webb-Mitchell, 2003). It was an activity that entailed hearing as much as seeing, for most reading was done aloud, often in the company of others. We might call this acoustical reading (for the importance of the acoustical dimension in Christian communication, see Webb, 2004). The lips were used as well as the eyes, and readers listened to the words pronounced, hearing, as Jean Leclercq says, the "voices of the pages," for "*legere* means at the same time *audire*": reading entailed hearing (Leclercq, 1978, p. 19). For the medievals, reading was both anticipated and reinforced by preceding and succeeding activities intended as continuous with the reading itself and with the rest of the Christian life. Reading could be considered a kind of rehearsal of the enjoyment of the goods or realities it spoke about. To meditate in the act of reading implied, as Leclercq (1978, p. 20) confirms, "thinking of a thing with the intent to do it; in other words, to prepare oneself for it, to prefigure it in the mind, to desire it, in a way, to do in advance, briefly, to practice it." Reading was an act of the whole being: it took place "with the body, since the mouth pronounced it, with the memory which fixes it, with the intelligence which understands its meaning and with the will which desires to put it into practice" (Leclercq, 1978, p. 22). A very common metaphor for reading was eating, sometimes described as mastication or rumination, for monasteries were dwelling places for mumblers and munchers of the word (Leclercq, 1978, p. 90; Illich, 1993, p. 56).

One of the leading works on reading in the Middle Ages was Hugh of St Victor's *Didascalion*, written in the 1120s at the abbey of St Victor near Paris. Hugh is a powerful representative of those many medieval writers who stressed the self-involving and transformational nature of reading in its role of relating us to God. Another example is Bernard of Clairvaux (see Sommerfeldt, 2004). For Hugh, learning, in which reading is a constitutive element, is an instrument in the restoration of divine wisdom in us. It orients us and moves us towards union with God. Learning and reading within this perspective combines intellectual, ethical and spiritual dimensions. Both effort and love are required if we are to progress in learning and in virtue. "Through concern you look ahead; through alertness you pay close attention" (Hugh, in Taylor, 1961, p. 100). In linking self-discipline with progress in reading and learning, Hugh quotes St Jerome, who pithily said, "A fat belly does not produce a fine perception" (Taylor, 1961, p. 100). He acknowledges that reading is not always benign in its effects on us, for the spirit can be afflicted, as well as helped, by study "through its quality, if the material has been too obscure, and through its quantity, if there has been too much of it" (Taylor, 1961, p. 130). At its best, however, reading and study will enable us to equip ourselves to respond worthily to God, constructing a life of grateful fidelity out of the gifts and graces showered on us. In another of his works Hugh says, "You shall build a house for the Lord out of your own self. He himself will be the builder; your heart will be the place; your thoughts will supply the material" (quoted by Taylor, 1961, p. 171). This is reminiscent of the admonition of Gregory the Great: "We ought to transform what we read into our very selves, so that when our mind is stirred by what it hears, our life may concur by practicing what has been heard" (Gregory, quoted by Taylor, 1961, p. 220).

One of the different emphases between reading (and learning) in the Middle Ages and in more recent times is a shift in the focus: instead of *sapientia* (wisdom) and *intelligentia* (understanding) being what is sought, it is *scientia* (knowledge) that is pursued. This shift indicates a move from one form of study to a significantly different type. In seeking *sapientia* or *intelligentia*, I stand *under* the material studied, accommodate myself obediently to its demands; I reach up to it as I seek to apprehend the world according to its categories. *Sapientia* or *intelligentia* is about understanding what comes to us from above us, from a higher level of being (and perfection). According to the medieval mentality, in pursuing *scientia* we investigate what is below us, a level of being that is inferior to us. Now what is studied is interrogated according to our categories, to satisfy our curiosity, in order to be amenable to our needs, to serve our purposes. Here we stand over the object of study. Understanding operates at a different level from overstanding. It calls upon some of the deeply personal and relatively passive qualities of the pilgrim seeker. To appreciate what comes to us from above requires waiting, patience, stillness and silence. It might be more accurate to describe these qualities, when operating conjointly, as comprising an active receptivity, a level of heightened attentiveness and contemplative capacity which depend upon discipline and training. With understanding it is my personal life that is very much in the laboratory, under scrutiny. There is no sharp separation in me among my moral, spiritual and intellectual dimensions. In the case of *scientia* I may be tempted to believe that my personal life is irrelevant to the progress of my studies, that it can be put aside when I am reading or investigating.

For the medievals, however, the goal of reading and study was wisdom and ultimately the beatific vision of God, gradually made possible via a growing capacity for spiritual apprehension, though this never occurs without God's grace, which precedes, accompanies and brings to perfection our feeble efforts. Holiness was considered an integral element in wisdom and the beatific vision, for faith in the truth and love of the good are united in God. Spiritual experience was not an optional extra but an essential feature of the most worthwhile studies. William of Auxerre, for example, writing in the early years of the thirteenth century, picked up the teaching in the Bible about the spiritual senses and developed this into a sophisticated analysis of how God uses our diverse capacities and desires to draw us to himself (Coolman, 2004). For William, as for so many other medievals, the gifts of the Holy Spirit are derived from Isaiah 11:2-3: wisdom, understanding, counsel, fortitude, knowledge, piety and fear of the Lord. These gifts lead us progressively from the exterior and active life (via fear, piety, knowledge, fortitude and counsel) to the interior, contemplative life (understanding and wisdom). For William, if spiritual apprehension is ever to be developed in us, it will call upon the wide range of our knowing capacities, capacities that are deeply enhanced or hindered by our virtues (or lack of them), as well as by the nature of our desires (what they are targeted on and the purchase they have on our lives). Knowledge of what is above us requires that we ascend, that our nature be transcended, that our wayward nature be brought into order, that our energies be focused, that we open ourselves to be made, by God, more similar to the divine nature.

This is a view of learning in which the intellectual, the moral, the aesthetic and the spiritual are shown to interact reciprocally. In a recent major study of the spiritual senses in the theology of William of Auxerre, Coolman (2004) shows how, for William, certain senses had to be developed and heightened in us if we are to have a chance to appreciate the nature of the divine. Human beings are created with the seeds of qualities that correspond with divine characteristics. If we are to perceive God's fullness (*plenitudine*), beauty (*pulchritude*), symphony (*simphonia*), good aroma (*bono odore*), pleasantness (*suavitas*) and sweetness (*dulcedo*), then we must learn how to delight in God through spiritual sight (*visus*), hearing (*auditus*), smell (*odoratus*), taste (*gustus*),and touch (*tactus*) (Coolman, 2004, p. 29). Some of these phrases, such as symphony and good aroma, might strike us as strange, perhaps too earthy, too literal, in relation to God. But I think that William, like so many of his contemporaries, was being realistic in believing that it was through harnessing, co-ordinating, disciplining and directing our God-given qualities and capacities that we would learn to read rightly not only the book of Scripture, but also the book of life as experienced in the world. William saw an essential resonance between what we have received and the One who gave these gifts to us. Wisdom and the vision of God, though coming to us as a gift that we could not merit, nevertheless came to us via the gifts we had already received, the inbuilt capacity to respond to God's call through the development of spiritual senses.

In all this, William expected a conjoining of faith with love, facilitated by an employment of our spiritual senses. "Charity desires, hungers for, pursues, effects, maintains, and augments that delight which occurs in faith's apprehension", while "faith cognizes, estimates, apprehends – in short, faith is *visus* [sight]. Charity desires, pursues, possesses, conjoins, rests – in short, charity is *tactus* [touch]" (Coolman, 2004, p. 149, 152). We have learned to be cautious about some forms of engaging the emotions in the process of religious communication, lest these slip into manipulation and reduce the freedom (and thus fail to take seriously the dignity) of the learner. However, William posits no sharp separation between the intellect, the will and the spiritual senses: each has a part to play; they belong together rather than being in conflict; each has a legitimate role in the path towards knowing God better. "Spiritual experience does not abandon doctrinal formulation; prior forms of knowing are not left behind by, or radically dissociated from, later forms .... *Scientia-cognoscere* structures and informs *sapientia-sentire*, while *sapientia-sentire* subsumes and consummates *scientia-cognoscere*" (Coolman, 2004, p. 5). To express this another way, the rigorous use of reason will guide our search, so that our findings will not be fanciful, the result of wish-fulfilment, but warranted by the evidence. At the same time, the deployment and development of our other capacities that can assist cognition, our virtues, our desires and our spiritual senses, can only enhance our use of reason, ensure it is an act of the whole person, press us to let our knowledge make a real difference in our lives, and open us up to respond to and to embrace the call and grace of God.

3. Beyond anaemic reading?

What I have described in section 2 is a more full-blooded, integrated approach to study than we are accustomed to now. It reminds us that how we read, and what we write for others to read, is inextricably linked to the kind of people we are. For the academic reader, too often "there is no moral relation between book and reader" (Griffiths, 2002, p. 38). Yet sacred scripture (e.g. 2 Pet 1:5-7) not only links knowledge to faith and virtue, as displayed in self-control, steadfastness, godliness and love, but also subordinates knowledge to these qualities. Such a view implies that "the intellect, the emotions, the will, the spirit and the body are all intricately connected and must all be continually purified" (Poplin, 2005, p. 169).

In a recent study of how theology was once taught in this more holistic way, as a pilgrimage towards God, one commentator says, "Reading is ... the activity of rightly ordering our desire towards its proper object" (Candler, 2006, p. 45). Such a statement is counter-intuitive in many educational contexts today, when skills and competencies are talked of as if they could be detached from the memories, motivations, character and relationships of learners, rather as software can be easily transferred between different kinds of hardware, unaffected by the host machine. A medieval reader's memory was trained in a liturgical setting, so that texts which were read were inextricably linked for readers with an "entire network of bodily movements, sounds, smells with which these readings were associated, as well as the time of day and season in which they were read" (Candler, 78). This is so different from our practice of private and silent reading, carried out as and when we please, and something quite separate for us from any fixed associations of location, surrounding activity, particular company or directed toward an enduring overriding purpose.

Our reading for study is expected to display objectivity, disinterest and detachment. It critiques, questions and interrogates the texts under review. It judges them by our criteria of relevance. Historical perspective and consciousness is often determinative of our interpretation. As David Williams says about the dominance of historical consciousness accompanying our reading, "We are no more the intended audience of the Bible than of Herodotus" (Williams, 2004, p. 53). The whole notion of attempting to read a text in accordance with the way it has been read throughout a tradition seems to strike right at the heart of the unfettered freedom of the reader. Of course, there is nothing wrong with reading that is influenced by our current preoccupations and interests, so long as we are not blinded by these to other possible readings and interpretations, ones that differ radically from, perhaps which challenge and even contradict, them.

What are the implications for Christian educators of my brief foray into past ways of approaching reading? My aim here is very modest. I believe that it is not our business to lament a lost past; nor is it helpful to lambast a deficient present. I do think we can show our students that the assumptions we bring to reading can make a significant difference to what we get out of it. We can propose to them that it is legitimate to consider a richer, more full-blooded and more holistic way of seeing their reading and their studies, as illustrated by some examples from the past. We can invite them to reflect on their own life and how the multiple dimensions of this might be influencing their reading, not only of texts in the traditional sense, of but also of their 'reading', reception or interpretation of all that happens to them and of all whom they meet. If it is true that "the inhabitants of a tradition enter its stories, enact its rituals, play its roles, explore its visions, try its arguments, feel its sensibilities" (Brown, 1994, p. 86), then standing at a distance, refusing to try out its perspectives, merely looking at a tradition, rather than through its spectacles, not allowing one's pattern of life to be challenged by it – all this will prevent our being able to read very deeply what it might have to offer us. It would be standing over what we study, but not standing within it. Such a stance might well prevent us reaching a worthwhile understanding.

In my experience of working with university students in recent years, I have begun the process of trying to help them to move from overstanding to understanding by inviting them to consider the factors that might be influencing their 'reading', interpreting the term very broadly. I simply suggest the following ten clusters of factors as worthy of consideration.

First, their experiences, memories and assumptions: what is the baggage (to use a negative term), or the equipment (for a more positive term) that they bring to the object of study? In some modules (both undergraduate and at Master's level) I invite students to reflect on how their past experience, whether in academic studies or their life experience more broadly, can either orient them towards or perhaps make them resistant to what we are going to study. I help them to see that they do not arrive in the class as a blank, without expectations or preliminary notions about the topic or the text. Chris Anderson, an English professor at Oregon State University and a Catholic Deacon, describes how he once conveyed to his students that "we all bring things to the text" by putting on his alb and stole in the classroom as he started to teach a class. In commenting on this activity of self-consciously dressing up in front of his students, Anderson quotes Northrop Frye that we live within "a body of assumptions and beliefs developed from our existential concerns" (Anderson, 2004, p. 27).

Second, their knowledge, maturity and intellectual capacity: rather than asking students to analyse these, I usually seek to get an initial sense of these for myself as teacher, through preliminary checking of what is known at the start of a course, although I invite them to recognise that each of us will bring a different and an uneven personal development to a task; we can be mature and confident in some respects, yet less so in others.

Third, their hopes and fears (and the state of their feelings more generally): at the start of a module, I invite students to acknowledge (even if only in their own minds) that we can easily be preoccupied with concerns outside of class that distract us from attending fully in the sessions, and that our hopes and fears for this module and the tasks associated with it could be well-founded or based on misunderstandings about what is required. They fairly easily accept that our energies for the forthcoming tasks can be reinforced and focused or dissipated and dispersed because of our personal emotional 'climate' – and that this may not be under our control. Cumulatively, consideration of these factors assists the students in becoming reflexive in their self-understanding and more aware of how they are relating to the reading to be tackled.

Fourth, their purposes and priorities (both short- and long-term): I invite students to connect the questions of the course with the questions of their lives and to see how strong links between these are likely to help their motivation in coping with the demands of the course.

Fifth, although I must be careful not to intrude into their privacy, or appear judgemental or puritanical about their lifestyle, I point out that what they are doing outside of class is likely to be as influential a factor in their progress as the kinds of learning they are engaged in with faculty at this time. Arriving in class after a late night's heavy drinking or partying might make participation in class or concentration on required reading in the library difficult.

Sixth, who they are with (i.e. the company they keep in and outside of class): if we all need a plausibility structure (to borrow a phrase from sociologist of religion Peter Berger) to support us in our various types of believing, then students should be conscious of how their pattern of friendships, affiliations and relationships both helps and hinders their work in class and their capacity to meet the demands of the course. Cumulatively, consideration of these factors suggests to the students that what is done in class is only the tip of the iceberg of their presence and participation: what appears on the surface is sustained by much more that lies beneath.

Seventh, their attitudes towards and relationship with the 'text' or speaker: in some cases students have encountered a lecturer in an earlier part of their studies, or they have already engaged with a text at a different level or for a different purpose than the one that pertains now. If the encounter with lecturer or text is new, it will still be mediated by initial impressions that 'frame' the engagement – for example, by the age, appearance, clothing, voice and bearing of the speaker; or by the appearance, font size, packaging and presentation of a text. Rather than focus on this at the start of a piece of work, I sometimes invite students to reflect at the end of a piece of work on how their relationship to speaker or text has changed in the period of study and to ask themselves to what degree initial impressions and expectations were met or modified in light of experience and what they would say to incoming students faced with the same speaker or text.

Eighth, the clarity and quality of the 'text': obviously, it must be acknowledged that this varies enormously; not all texts will prove accessible, interesting or relevant to any particular group of students. What 'gets through' to one student might not to another. To consider this factor is to recognize that not all progress or setbacks in our 'reading' can be attributed to the subjective conditions of the learner.

Ninth, chance and unforeseen circumstances and connections: these can make a significant difference in how individual students or even a whole class receive a text. A personal tragedy, a political crisis, a popular song in the charts, and a host of trivial and serious life experiences can trigger associations between student and text that could not have been foreseen by them or by their teacher. Rosenblatt puts it thus: "The same text will have a different meaning and value to us at different times or under different circumstances because some state of mind, a worry, a temperamental bias, or a contemporary social crisis may make us especially receptive or especially impervious to what the work offers" (as quoted by Pike, 2003, p. 44). To be inattentive to the operation of serendipity and calamity in our responses to texts and the resonances they might have for us would be to treat teaching and learning as a process that is logical, automatic and predictable, whereas in practice it is often wonderful, dramatic and escapes our most careful attempts to chart its progress.

Cumulatively, consideration of these factors brings home to students the need for an appreciation of the complexity of (and mutual interaction between) the tasks of learning and need for attaining some meta-cognitive perspective on their progress. Crude judgements, such as "this [activity] is stupid", "I can't do this" or "this text is impossible" are less likely to be made; while a comment such as "this is what I think is happening that is affecting my learning (positively and negatively)" is more likely.

Tenth, I suggest to students that our character, with its moral and spiritual dimensions, can make a difference to the effectiveness of our studies. Qualities such as persistence, readiness to accept correction, humility, patience, courage, willingness to co-operate, self-discipline and commitment can create the conditions for successful study. By bringing together the character of the student with the 'character' of a text, I try to encourage students to question how what they are saying, assuming, valuing, privileging, neglecting, downgrading, and what they are committed to relates to what the text is advocating, displaying, revealing, ignoring, critiquing, and taking for granted. By the time they have got to my tenth factor influencing reading, they are beginning to be open to the possibility of expanding their appreciation of what real reading might require of them. Even if they do not wish to take that journey very far, they are less likely to over-rate the quality or to exaggerate the value of the reading they have done, and they are more willing to see the potential connections between their personal and their academic lives. This is not to be inside the world of faith, but it might encourage them to cross the threshold which divides overstanding from understanding.

Bibliography

Anderson, C. (2004). *Teaching as believing.* Waco, TX: Baylor University Press.

Brown, D. (1994). *Boundaries of our habitations.* New York: SUNY Press.

Candler, P. (2006). *Theology, rhetoric, manuduction, or reading Scripture together on the path to God.* Grand Rapids, MI: Eerdmans.

Cavallo, G., & Chartier, R. (2003). *A history of reading in the West.* Cambridge: Polity Press.

Coolman, B. T. (2004). *Knowing God by experience.* Washington, DC: The Catholic University of America Press.

Griffiths, P. (1999). *Religious reading.* New York: Oxford University Press.

Griffiths, P. (2002). Reading as a spiritual discipline. In G. Jones, & S. Paulsell (Eds.), *The scope of our art: The vocation of the theological teacher* (pp. 32-47). Grand Rapids, MI: Eerdmans.

Illich, I. (1993). *In the vineyard of the text.* Chicago: University of Chicago Press.

Kivy, P. (2006). *The performance of reading.* Oxford: Blackwell.

Leclercq, J. (1978). *The love of learning and the desire for God.* London: SPCK.

MacInnis, J. (2002). Theological education as formation for ministry. In R. Petersen, & N. Rourke (Eds.), *Theological literacy for the twenty-first century.* Grand Rapids, MI: Eerdmans.

Pike, M. (2003). The Bible and the reader's response. *Journal of Education & Christian Belief,* 7(1), 37-51.

Pike, M. (2006). From beliefs to skills: The secularization of literacy and the moral development of citizens. *Journal of Beliefs & Values, 27*(3), 281-289.

Poplin, M. (2005). The radical call to service: The five tasks. In J. M. Dunaway (Ed.), *Gladly learn, gladly teach*. Macon, GA: Mercer University Press, 146-171.

Purves, A. (1998). *The web of text and the web of God*. New York: The Guilford Press.

Rosenblatt, L. (1978). *The reader, the text, the poem: The transactional theory of the literary work*. Carbondale, IL: Southern Illinois University Press.

Rush, O. (1997). *The reception of doctrine: An appropriation of Hans Robert Jauss' reception aesthetics and literary hermeneutics*. Rome: Editrice Pontifica Universita Gregoriana.

Smith, D. I. (2004). The poet, the child and the blackbird: Aesthetic reading and spiritual development. *International Journal of Children's Spirituality, 9*(2), 143-154.

Sommerfeldt, J. (2004). *Bernard of Clairvaux on the life of the mind*. New York: The Newman Press.

Stock, B. (1996). *Augustine the reader*. Cambridge, MA: Harvard University Press.

Taylor, J. (Trans. and ed.). (1961). *The Didascalion of Hugh of Saint Victor*. New York: Columbia University Press.

Von Hügel, F. (1926). *Essays & addresses on the philosophy of religion. Second series*. London: Dent.

Webb, S. (2004). *The divine voice*. Grand Rapids, MI: Brazos Press.

Webb-Mitchell, B. (2003). *Christly gestures*. Grand Rapids, MI: Eerdmans.

Williams, D. (2004). *Receiving the Bible in faith*. Washington, DC: Catholic University of America Press.

JE&CB 11:2 (2007) 39-52   1366-5456

C. Rebecca Rine

Learning to Read with Augustine
of Hippo

THE CONFESSIONS OF Augustine of Hippo can be read as a lesson in reading, one in which Augustine teaches by example as well as precept. Throughout this work, the relationship between faith and reading is clearly on Augustine's mind, as is his desire to teach others what he has learned. As we consider our own approaches to the confluence of faith, reading, and teaching, we have much to learn from Augustine's narrative self-portrait of himself as reader. After reviewing aspects of this self-portrait, its implications for Augustine's approach to reading and for our own reading and teaching practices are considered.

As Augustine of Hippo writes his *Confessions*, he speculates that only a "tiny part" of the human race will read his words (Augustine, 1991, II.iii.5). Although this may be true in one sense – many people have never read or even heard of Augustine – we can safely suppose that the quantity of Augustine's readership has far exceeded his expectations.[1] Many generations of students, believers and skeptics alike, have read and commented this text. The *Confessions* have been (and will be) read as philosophy, theology, autobiography, devotional work, and prayer; they encompass and surpass each of these.

Peter Candler (2006) notes that the *Confessions* provide an itinerary for readers: "[In the *Confessions*] Augustine has in mind not just the transferal of autobiographical information to the reader, but her transformation. Augustine, it seems, hopes for his readers to repeat, non-identically, his own itinerary ..." (p. 53). Augustine seems to confirm this characterization as he wonders aloud if he is misleading his readers; he clearly envisions himself as leader and his readers as followers (XIII. xx.27). In Book XI, Augustine addresses God with this explanation for his writing: "Why then do I set before you an ordered account of so many things? It is certainly not through me that you know them. But I am stirring up love for you in myself and in those who read this, so that we may all say, 'Great is the Lord and highly worthy to be praised'" (XI.i.1).

And so, it seems that Augustine is trying to take us somewhere with his writing. But when we follow the path of the *Confessions*, we see that before Augustine was a writer, he was a reader – a reader of Scripture and of other texts that informed his interaction with Scripture. Indeed, he was a reader not only of texts, but of everything he experienced. As he writes, he offers us interpretations of interpretive traditions, and readings of others' writings, pointing the way forward for other readers who, like himself, have not always found reading to be comfortable or immediately rewarding.

The *Confessions*, then, can also be read as a lesson in reading, one in which Augustine teaches by example as well as precept. Throughout this work, the relationship between faith and reading is clearly on his mind, as is his desire to teach others what he has learned.[2] As we consider our own approaches to the confluence of faith, reading, and teaching, we have much to learn from Augustine's narrative self-portrait of himself as reader. After reviewing aspects of this self-portrait, we will consider its implications for Augustine's approach to reading and for our own reading and teaching practices.

Reading in the *Confessions*

The theme of reading is prevalent throughout the *Confessions*. Though the related theme of speech or language (particularly the ineffable) has drawn much scholarly attention, consideration of reading itself is often limited to Augustine's conversion narrative.[3] In this scene, while bitterly weeping in a state of spiritual indecision, Augustine hears a child chanting, "*Tolle, lege*," or "Take, read." He opens Paul's letters and reads the first passage he encounters. Convicted by the admonitions of Romans 13:13-14, he recalls that "with the last words of this sentence, it was as if a light of relief from all anxiety flooded into my heart" (VIII.xii.29). Thus, after years of struggle, a single instance of unpremeditated, indiscriminate[4] reading results in Augustine's conversion. While those who have profited from his participation in the church are no doubt thankful for Augustine's experience, it does not necessarily provide a useful model for us as we think about how to teach reading.[5] Whether we view his action as random selection or Spirit-led discovery, we do not find here a method of reading that can be reliably transmitted to others.

The account of Augustine's conversion may be the best-known story about reading in the *Confessions*, but it is not the only one worthy of attention. Augustine narrates his experiences as reader from his earliest school days, when he was forced to read the Greek and Latin literary classics as part of the standard curriculum. At first, he has "no love" for reading books (I.xii.19), and by the time he reaches Carthage, he is more interested in the style of a work than its ideas. But prompted by his reading of Cicero's *Hortensius*, he soon matures into a seeker of truth wherever it may be found (III.iv.7-8). Augustine puts his faith in the writings of the Manichees, who promise to dispel all errors. This claim is proven false when Augustine becomes increasingly aware of the inadequacies of Manichean beliefs, and he soon loses respect for the proponents of Manichaeism (especially the much-touted Faustus).

To this point, though Augustine has been familiar with the Christian scriptures from childhood, he regards them as difficult and obscure – certainly not a source of spiritual or literary guidance. His disappointing encounter with the Manichees, however, causes him to reconsider elements of the Christian faith. Realizing that the Christian perspective at least *could* be true, even though he himself does not yet know *whether* it is true, Augustine hears the preaching of Ambrose, from whom he learns how to use the principles of figurative interpretation. This way of reading gives him an alternative perspective on the apparent difficulties in reading Scripture. Yet still he does not believe. He continues to read Scripture alongside literature from other branches of knowledge (philosophy, science, history, etc.). Then, while conversing with Simplicianus, Augustine learns about Victorianus, a well-liked and highly accomplished tutor to senators who had come to Christ through his reading of philosophy and Scripture. Augustine is moved by this story and acknowledges that the Christian gospel is true; nevertheless, due to fear and sinful attachments, he is not yet moved to act on his professed beliefs.

It takes another reader, and another account of a converted reader, to bring Augustine to his knees. This reader is Ponticianus, a stranger who visits Augustine to complete some business affairs. Ponticianus notices that Augustine is reading the works of Paul and reveals that he (Ponticianus) is a baptized believer. He conveys the story of Antony the monk, who heard Scripture read aloud and was converted. Ponticianus recounts how two of his friends had read Antony's story and had likewise committed themselves to Christ. These stories remind Augustine of the significant change in his own life that came about as a result of reading, namely his commitment to seek truth after reading the *Hortensius* at the age of 19. As he laments over his failure to keep this commitment, he recalls the infamous prayer of his youth: "Grant me chastity and continence, but not yet" (VIII.vii.17). Tormented by the war of wills within him, he begins to weep. And while he is weeping he hears the command to "Take, read," and in desperation, he obeys.

As the post-conversion narrative unfolds, Augustine does not leave behind the theme of reading. He describes renewed experiences of reading Scripture, this time with fuller understanding. He reflects on reading and interpretation, particularly with regard to Scripture, and repeatedly mentions his dependence on God for aid in understanding. In a culminating passage of Book XIII, God is depicted as a book read by the angels; his word is eternal even though his preachers pass away (XIII.xv.18). The final sentences of the *Confessions* declare that not humans or angels, but only God, can ensure that a person will understand or interpret appropriately. Thus, the *Confessions* end where they began, with faith that yields both understanding and praise.

Learning How to Read

The significance of Augustine's conversion scene, though weighty in its own right, is much better understood in light of these additional reading-related scenes in the *Confessions*. The reading motif in the *Confessions* reveals the complex yet central role of reading during every stage of Augustine's personal development. As we might, Augustine acknowledges the possibility of Spirit-led moments of insight, particularly during the reading of Scripture. But he also urges believers not to assume that all reading is directly guided by divine revelation.[6] In the prologue to *On Christian Teaching*, Augustine argues that the potential for divine intervention does not negate the need for human effort in learning how to read faithfully. In fact, teaching others to read is not only possible, but necessary. As he quite eloquently puts it, "Everything which does not decrease on being given away is not properly owned when it is owned and not given" (Augustine, 1999, p. 8). The ability to read, and read well, clearly falls into this category.

This assertion, though potentially valid, is still insufficient to guide us. It is not enough to believe that faithful reading can and should be taught; the question we must answer is, how? What is meant by "faithful" reading – faithful to what? How can we encourage our students, in whatever discipline, from whatever background, in whatever state of belief or disbelief, to become more faithful readers? How should we read, and how should we teach others to do so? The passages cited above, as well as others in the *Confessions*, suggest the following: for Augustine, "faithful" or "Christian" reading is goal-oriented and is learned through willful pursuit over time, through a process of trial and error, in the company of other readers. None of these elements is sufficient on its own, but together they provide a framework for understanding the task of Christian readers and teachers of reading.

Goal-Oriented Reading

Those who have read *On Christian Teaching* will be familiar with Augustine's reliance on a key distinction between things that are to be used and things that are to be enjoyed (1999, p. 9). His hermeneutical system depends on the belief that only the Trinity is to be truly enjoyed, or loved. Everything else – including other people, angels, objects, and the like – are to be either enjoyed and used, or simply used. Thus, the proper end of living is the love of God, which is sometimes expressed through the love of neighbor. Orientation to this way of thinking is essential for understanding: "Whoever, therefore, thinks that he understands the divine Scriptures or any part of them so that it does not build the double love of God and of our neighbor does not understand it at all" (Augustine, 1999, p. 30). As David Lyle Jeffrey (1996) summarizes, "For Augustine the Christian student is one whose efforts always begin in a desire to obey the Great Commandment: progressing in a process of patient and laborious refinement of insight, they end in obedience as well" (p. 87). Jeffrey goes on to contrast useful and useless reading, the former being characterized by charity but the latter springing from cupidity (p. 88). Augustine's teleological focus on love pervades his interpretation theory.

What Augustine articulates in *On Christian Teaching*, he demonstrates in the *Confessions*. Though he could not see it at the time, his various experiences of reading (not only Scripture but also philosophy, the Manichees, etc.) are leading him to love God more. He is progressively initiated into a Christian form of reading that finds its path and its goal in God. Reflecting on the reasons that God might have allowed him to read philosophy before he fully appreciated Scripture, Augustine gives the following account:

> I believe that you wanted me to encounter [the Platonists' books] before I came to study your scriptures. Your intention was that the manner in which I was affected by them should be imprinted in my memory, so that when later I had been made docile by your books and my wounds were healed by your gentle fingers, I would learn to discern and distinguish the difference between presumption and confession, between those who see what the goal is but not how to get there and those who see the way which leads to the home of bliss, not merely as an end to be perceived but as a realm to live in. (VII.xx.26)

In sum, Augustine believes that the writings of the Platonists led him to desire truth. But this desire, as any desire, could not be fulfilled unless it was properly oriented to Christian love. Thirst for knowledge only leads to pride; without the truth of Scripture to contextualize his desire, he lacks "the charity which builds on the foundation of humility, which is Christ Jesus" (VII.xx.26). Once he learns the proper goal of Christian reading (that is, greater love for God), he understands that his passions were formerly misdirected and therefore mislead-ing, allowing him to perceive but not pursue his proper goal. Now, passion for truth has been replaced by love for God. Pride has been replaced by humility. But Augustine's past is still with him in a sense, present in his memory and reminding him to acknowledge his perpetual dependence on God. This dependence, which enables love, is required of all true readers.

Willful Pursuit over Time

According to Augustine, his improvement as a reader is due not only to his willful pursuit of truth (which is far from consistent) but also to God's willful pursuit of him. Throughout young adulthood Augustine searches for writings that will satisfy his intellect and spirit. He reads the works of Aristotle without an exposi-tor and nevertheless understands them. He engages his friends in discussion of key works and always hopes to find better texts to read. This persistence, though laudable, is not enough to lead him to the truth. Augustine describes how blind he was to the truth that God was revealing:

> What advantage came to me from the fact that I had by myself read and understood all the books I could get hold of on the arts which they call liberal, at a time when I was the most wicked slave of evil lusts? I enjoyed reading them, though I did not know the source of what was true and certain in them. I had my back to the light and my face towards the things which are illuminated. So my face, by which I was enabled to see the things lit up, was not itself illuminated. (IV. xvi.30)

Here, again, we see Augustine struggling with misplaced passions or "evil lusts," which hold him captive. Noting his own helplessness to improve his posi-tion, Augustine affirms that God's seeking of him preceded his seeking of God (V.ii.2). Augustine admits to God that "I did not know what you were doing with me," but later he comes to read each experience, even apparent punishments or evils, as part of God's plan to bring Augustine to him (III.iv.8). As Karl Morrison (1992) summarizes, "Augustine took great pains to assert that God had presided over his conversion at every stage, and, in fact, that God was, in some sense, the coauthor of the *Confessions*" (p. 10). Reading, then, is learned through both divine activity and human effort; both are important for maturation.

Not surprisingly, though perhaps disappointingly for some, the divine way of teaching is not an instantaneous one. Augustine's progression as a reader takes years, even decades, to become evident. As we follow his story, changes usually occur incrementally, rarely in leaps and bounds – and rarely within the span of time known to us as a semester or school year. The closing remarks of the *Con-*

fessions reveal that the process is ongoing even as Augustine completes his narrative, for he reiterates his dependence on God for further understanding (XII. xxxviii.53). Augustine's emphasis on the deliberate yet purposeful work of God reminds us that learning to read is a lifelong process.

Trial and Error

Learning to read is also a circuitous process. We see this most clearly as we watch Augustine struggle with Scripture. Even after coming to faith in Christ and acknowledging the worth of Scripture, Augustine constantly wrestles with its meaning. He is at pains to account for its literary style, which is distinct from the accepted norms of the literary "greats." In the pages of the *Confessions* and again in *On Christian Teaching*, Augustine formulates a sophisticated apologetic for Scripture, viewing it as open to the lowly but closed to the proud. He now reads the obscurities of Scripture as a sign of God's purposeful work.

Augustine is profoundly aware of the potential implications of competing interpretations of the same text and of the ultimate inadequacy of language to express what is most important. He is concerned with the nature of inspiration, the challenges of translation, and guidelines for interpretation. At no point does he "arrive" in his reading of Scripture, and on particularly difficult points he qualifies his understanding as "provisional" and open-ended rather than complete and final. For instance, in Book XII of the *Confessions*, Augustine engages his opponents on the interpretation of Genesis 1. He expounds and defends his own views against the Manichees and other believers who differ with him. In the end, he says, "With those … who honour your holy scripture written by that holy man Moses and agree with us that we should follow its supreme authority, but who on some point contradict us, my position is this: You, our God, shall be arbiter between my confessions and their contradictions" (XII.xvi.23). For Augustine, there is no "God's-eye view" accessible to humans through which we can adjudicate among readings with absolute certainty. This is all the more reason for championing the standard of love. Those who focus on the love of God and neighbor in all of their readings are better able to suspend judgment on disputed points, offering their preferred response while granting the possibility of legitimate alternatives.

Recognizing that the ability to read well comes only through trial and error – through trying, failing, and trying again – Augustine advocates an attitude of humility for readers and teachers alike. This attitude prepares readers for the fourth and final element of Christian reading, that is, reading in community.

A Company of Readers

We have already seen how important other readers are in helping Augustine to learn how (and how not) to read. Debating with friends, questioning experienced readers, and seeking new authors as companions are all part of his education in reading. One of the most influential readers in Augustine's life is the bishop Ambrose. Ambrose himself had once read and copied by hand the writings of the Manichees that Augustine found so intriguing. Yet Ambrose, through this reading, had rejected these writings and turned to God. When Augustine's mother, Monica, beseeches Ambrose to intervene in the life of her wayward son, Ambrose responds as a reader who recognizes the needs of another reader: "'Let him be where he is,' he said; 'only pray the Lord for him. By his reading he will discover what an error and how vast an impiety it all is'" (III.xii.21). In hindsight, these words seem almost prophetic.

Not only Monica and Ambrose, but also Augustine's peers assist him in learning how to read. In fact, attesting to his friends' significance in his development as a reader, Augustine writes more extensively about Nebridius and Alypsius than about anyone else, including his mother or mentors (Voiku, 1997, p. 47). Augustine's narrative speaks to the power of readers to influence each other, concerning both what and how to read. His writings remind us that the company we keep as readers will affect our reading; reading, though often done in private, is not a solitary activity.

Teaching How to Read

What are the implications of these categories for pedagogy? With Augustine for our reading instructor and his *Confessions* for our primer, we are inspired to ponder our own reading and teaching practices as instances of faith, passion, and spiritual transformation. The applications offered below are, of course, not exhaustive.

Goal-Oriented Teaching

When we acknowledge the significance of goals in the process of teaching and reading, we recognize that one way of defining Christian teaching or reading is to say that these activities must be oriented around Christian goals. Of course, this only shifts the debate rather than ending it, for not everyone will agree about what constitutes a properly Christian goal.[7] As our reading of Augustine shows, he believed that the primary Christian goal in reading and in life should be the double love of God and neighbor. The prominence of love in Augustine's hermeneutic suggests that for him, good reading is passionate reading, engaging both heart and mind. Reading involves the whole person, for love is not simply an emotion, nor is it purely intellectual. Body,[8] mind, will, and passions are combined in this hermeneutic of love.

Our educational contexts and personal values will influence the ways we incorporate "loving God and neighbor" into our teaching practices. An ongoing question for the contemporary professor is whether or not, or to what extent, the academic and social norms of the American university are compatible with the norm of Christian love that Augustine advocates. But no matter the situation on any given campus, we cannot assume that our students will be believers in Christ, nor can we ignore the reality that each student holds beliefs about the value of religion. For those who practice the teaching profession as an act of love, the best means of loving in any given situation must be constantly reevaluated. Perpetual reevaluation is needed in any setting, not just in the university.

We must also consider what it means to read lovingly, or to practice charitable reading.[9] The ways we introduce assignments, relate class time to readings, and expect our students to engage with the material all teach the students how to read. These activities, while having little to do with any particular text, reveal more about our goals (loving or not) than we might think. Augustine read a great deal before he recognized that loving God and neighbor was the one goal he should be pursuing. Our students may or may not be pursuing a specific goal in their reading, but part of teaching students to read is teaching them to distinguish the worth of various goals and to competently pursue particular goals as readers. Helping students define their own attitudes and goals when reading a text is also an important step in developing shared goals within a class. Student feedback may be gathered anonymously, using written surveys or short answer question-naires, or face-to-face, through informal interviews or focus groups. All of this is accomplished as we craft our reading assignments and assessments, which help to determine both actual and perceived goals in the classroom.

Willful Pursuit over Time

This category consists of three elements: human effort, divine activity, and the passage of time. As stated earlier, for Augustine, learners only begin learning when they adopt a spirit of humility. Christian teachers of reading must adopt this spirit for ourselves and urge our students to do the same. As co-learners with our students, we can nurture our own humility through prayer, in which we ac-knowledge God's existence and relationship to us. In a Christian classroom, we can encourage our students to explore the relationship between prayer and read-ing. In any classroom, we can help students articulate their perception of what it means to read with humility, and discuss why this may or may not be important.

As responsible teachers of reading, we must carefully guide both *what* and *how* our students read. Our selection of certain texts or even editions of texts speaks to our values. But our work does not stop there. We sometimes neglect to engage our students about their approaches to texts both ancient and modern. Whether we are teaching in the arts and sciences, schools of education, law schools, medical schools, or another context, we can increase our students' interpretive sophistica-tion by defamiliarizing the ways of reading that dominate or subtly influence our discipline. To take just one example, if we were to assign Augustine's *Confessions* in class, we would do well to discuss the potential differences between modern and medieval ways of reading. Brian Stock (2001) comments:

> Contemporary criticism has considerably obscured the relationship between reading and contemplative practice that was deliberately in-corporated into many late ancient and medieval writings on the self. As a result, as new generation of readers has largely been deprived of the historical disciplines that are needed to attain an understanding of this poetry of the inner life. (p. 23)

If this statement is accurate, it would certainly be relevant to contemporary interpretations of the text, even if contemporary interpretations self-consciously preferred *not* to employ historical disciplines in the reading of the text. By facili-tating discussions with students about ways and levels of reading, we can enrich their experience and understanding of what reading might entail (see also Sul-livan, this volume).

According to Augustine's account, God's role in a person's journey as reader is much greater than that person's own role. It is also largely imperceptible. This realization can prompt at least two responses from those of us who are trying to teach others how to read. First, it can predispose us to listen to God before we speak to others. Augustine meditates on the "listening" aspect of prayer: "Your best servant is the person who does not attend so much to hearing what he himself wants as to willing what he has heard from you" (X.xxvi.37). The spirit of listening, of course, is one that proves beneficial in our relationship not just with God but also with other people, including our students. Second, this reality calls us to greater faith. The fact that we cannot see immediate results in our students' lives does not mean that God is not working. In fact, God calls us to affirm that he is working, even and especially when we cannot see it. This faith enables greater understanding, as Augustine says: "[Let the one seeking you] rejoice and delight in finding you who are beyond discovery rather than fail to find you by supposing you to be discoverable" (I.vi.10). Our faith in God opens rather than closes the paths to knowing him; it does the same for our students.

Being "full of faith" also requires a measure of patience and a willingness to persevere even though the only certainty seems to be the perpetual presence of uncertainty. We will not always see the fruit of our labor in the classroom or elsewhere; in fact, we usually do not see it. Knowing that people learn to read over a lifetime, we can be confident that the seeds we plant will one day be watered, and that God will give the increase.

Trial and Error

Sometimes we think of "trial and error" as a process antithetical to receiving guidance. If this were true, then the role of the teacher in learning would be minimal. In some ways, this *is* true. As teachers, we cannot learn "for" our students, or force them to learn. Nevertheless, we can point out the most likely path to learning. Some trials, as some errors, are not worth repeating. Others must be experienced by each of us. Seeking to offer guidance, teachers can learn another lesson from Augustine, this time from the way he crafts the *Confessions*. Pierre Hadot (1995) notes that ancient philosophers served as spiritual directors for their pupils:

> [Works such as the *Confessions* were] written not so much to inform the reader of a doctrinal content but to form him, to make him traverse a certain itinerary in the course of which he will make spiritual progress. This procedure is clear in the works of Plotinus and Augustine, in which all the detours, starts and stops, and digressions of the work are formative elements. (p. 64)

The direction we provide in the classroom may exhibit similar features. Knowing that trial and error is a natural part of learning, we can adapt our teaching in light of particular students' capabilities and motivations. Differentiated learning techniques are a contemporary manifestation of a pedagogy based on sensitivity to differences among students. What this theory does *not* generally account for is the spirituality of our students – the very thing that ancient philosophers found essential to instruction. Susan Handelman explores these issues in an intriguing chapter on "Stopping the Heart." Handelman (2002) writes of her own struggle over how to "bring a discourse of – for want of a better term – 'spirituality' to [the] classroom without sacrificing [the] goals of challenging critical thinking and the free play of ideas" (p. 205). She acknowledges that the very things which drive us to study a certain subject are often hidden when we teach (or learn), and she describes her own efforts to bring those aspects into play without sacrificing intellectual integrity. Arguing that "the teaching that is truly received and absorbed by the student is done via indirection," Handelman suggests that we need not express religious beliefs or personal passions in a direct way, but that we are responsible to create a space for such expression should students desire it. That is, the class should be open to such concerns, because they are so essential to the make-up of human beings. The compelling nature of her argument may not make her ideas any easier to implement, but it does give us important food for thought. If Hadot is right, and Augustine was practicing a similar style of indirection throughout the *Confessions*, then we perhaps can begin to envision what such an approach might look like.

A Company of Readers

> Preachers, teachers, mothers – other people – that is how God chooses to teach us. Other people teach us to speak and to read in the first place and other people subsequently teach us to speak and read and sing the things of God. Our teaching of one another is one of these divinely intended ligatures of love. (Soskice, 2002, p. 450)

These words from philosophical theologian Janet Soskice encapsulate her analysis of what she calls Augustine's "profoundly social religious epistemology" (p. 450). Augustine's narrative shows how we learn from one another without even realizing it. One of the best things we can do as teachers is to embrace the full potential of this social epistemology as it relates to the practice of reading. When we cultivate the company of readers within our classroom to its full potential, we make good use of the resources at hand. This may involve presenting our own ways of reading as models for others, as well as allowing students to model their reading styles for each other.

John C. Cavadini (2004) suggests that Augustine adopts a similar tactic in his many sermons to the public. Augustine delivers his sermons as "acts of inquiry, as instances of seeking understanding of Scripture" (p. 73). This inquiry is not just Augustine's: he invites his audience to accompany him on the path of discovery (p. 75). Through these rhetorical stances, Augustine comes alongside his listeners rather than preaching down to them from above. He uses the same technique in *De Trinitate*, one of the most complex of his doctrinal works. Cavadini observes that the key difference between Augustine's sermons and *De Trinitate* is that in the former, he appeals primarily to the faith that he and his hearers share, whereas in the latter, he relies on the training in the liberal arts that he and his readers share (p. 81).[10] In each case, he presents himself as a model inquirer and expects his listeners to follow.

Just as Augustine provided a model of inquiry and interpretation for his listeners, we can provide such a model for our students – and encourage them to become models for others. Modeling is a significant yet underutilized approach to the teaching of reading. One way of becoming a model reader is by narrating our responses to a particular text even as we are reading it. This technique is also useful when teaching others to write. How might this look in the classroom? While everyone is looking at the same text, teachers or students can verbalize their impressions of the title, first paragraph, main argument, and so on. When we make visible our internal reading processes, we help students think about their own reading processes. Modeling can extend beyond our personal responses to imagined responses of people from other perspectives. Students who do not feel comfortable speaking about their own feelings may be willing to talk about how an imagined reader (of whatever description we deem best) might respond. Creating an environment that encourages multiple responses to a given text helps develop evaluative skills and emphasizes the role of community in creating and sustaining meaning.

We can also encourage students to expand their reading repertoire and share their reading with others, thus embodying the social epistemology recounted by Augustine. In many ways, this social epistemology goes against the individual accountability that permeates American education. However, since the 1970s and the introduction of open admissions policies in American universities, teachers have expressed increasing interest in collaborative methods (Howard, 2001, p. 54).

One of the easiest ways to reinforce a social epistemology is in reading assignments, because students are not evaluated for reading in the same way that they are for writing.[11] Collaborative methods might include reading discussion groups, either during or outside of class, which require students to gather around an assigned or self-selected text. Another means of creating community in the classroom, without expecting spontaneous reading performances, is to ask students to write about their readings before coming to class. Sharing and discussing these writings provides access to multiple ways of approaching a text. Finally, assignments such as annotated bibliographies or producing a top ten list of significant authors in a given field are also useful in prompting students to consider the full extent of the company of readers surrounding them. These readers include the teacher, other students, and other writers who are not present.[12] Once several voices have been included in the discussion, it may be worthwhile to evaluate their relative value or usefulness for reading the text at hand. After all, if social epistemology describes how we learn, then the people we learn from and with play an important role in what we learn. Learning to discriminate between desirable and undesirable influences is part of learning how to read well.

Concluding Thoughts

Our investigation of Augustine's works has uncovered a potential model for reading and the teaching of reading, yet this model is not far removed from more general descriptions of the Christian life. Not surprisingly, there is significant overlap between Adler and Van Doren's *How to Read a Book* and David McKenna's *How to Read a Christian Book*. This leads us to ask what, if any, difference there would be between the contents of a book entitled *How to Be a Christian Reader* and the more general *How to Be a Christian*. In the end, what seems to be required for reader and teacher alike is faith in God, the cultivation of the fruit of the Spirit, and fellowship with a select cloud of witnesses. Many of the insights that Augustine offers are not altogether unfamiliar to us, but it is only when we are reminded of these basic ideas that we realize how easy it is to overlook what is most familiar.

This exploration of Augustine's approach to reading, while limited in scope, should spur us to further study. Although the quantity of Augustine's readership over time may have far exceeded his initial expectations, we are left to wonder how he would regard the quality of his readers over the ages. He clearly believes that the quality of his own reading improved over time, and he calls other readers to continue their quests for deeper and better reading of Scripture and of everything they experience – even if that quest brings confusion and difficulty at various points. Whether we enjoy lengthy friendship or only a cursory acquaintance with Augustine's works, we find that reading Augustine can make us better readers, and help us think about the relationship of faith, reading, and teaching.

Notes

1   This is likely the case even if Augustine's disclaimer was made in jest, or false humility.

2   This is also true of Augustine's more theoretical *On Christian Teaching*.

3   Two notable exceptions are Brian Stock's *Augustine the Reader* (1998) and *After Augustine: The Meditative Reader and the Text* (2001), which address Augustine's approach to reading in a wide range of his works.

4   Indiscriminate in a limited sense, for Augustine exercises discrimination in his choice to read the Christian scriptures instead of another text.

5   Though some of us have wished that it might. See Nussbaum (1990) p. 319 for a scene dominated by longing for a "Tolle, lege" experience.

6   For Augustine's defense of the need to teach others, see *On Christian Teaching* (1999) pp. 4-6.

7   A good starting point for this discussion is found in Leland Ryken's *The Liberated Imagination: Thinking Christianly About the Arts* (1989). While Ryken's subject extends beyond literature to all forms of art, he provides key categories for analysis, particularly in chapter seven, "What is Christian Art?" Ryken discusses common fallacies in defining and evaluating "Christian" art and artists.

8   On first glance, the inclusion of "body" in Augustine's concerns might seem out of step with his Neoplatonist tendencies, which may devalue the body. However, Augustine includes descriptions of the physical act of reading at several points in the *Confessions*. For a fuller discussion of kinesthetic elements of reading in the *Confessions*, see Morrison (1992) pp. 26-29.

9   What it means to read charitably, either for Augustine or for us, is far from clear. Alan Jacobs (2001) observes that "an account of the hermeneutics of love is one of the great unwritten chapters in the history of Christian theology" (p. 26). See also Jacobs, this volume, for further reflection on charitable reading and teaching.

10   This insight may provide a partial answer to the question "how might a Christian's teaching be different in a religious versus a non-religious context?"

11   When writing, students are always supposed to credit their sources. However, everything they write is coming from some kind of source – perhaps one that is more

removed than the books in front of them, but nevertheless is influential in their thinking. It becomes impossible to document everything. This is one of the difficulties of a writing culture that conceives ideas as intellectual property when in fact most of the "property" is shared.

12   For more on collaborative pedagogy and its implications for education, see Lunsford (2001) and Murphy (2001).

Bibliography

Adler, M. J., & Van Doren, C. (1997). *How to read a book*. New York: Simon and Schuster.

Augustine. (1991). *Confessions* (H. Chadwick, Trans.). New York: Oxford University Press.

Augustine. (1999). *On Christian teaching* (R. P. H. Green, Trans.). New York: Oxford University Press.

Candler, Jr., P. M. (2006). *Theology, rhetoric, manuduction, or reading Scripture together on the path to God*. Grand Rapids, MI: William B. Eerdmans.

Cavadini, J. C. (2004). Simplifying Augustine. In J. Van Engen (Ed.), *Educating people of faith: Exploring the history of Jewish and Christian communities* (pp. 63-84). Grand Rapids, MI: William B. Eerdmans.

Gallagher, S. V. & Lundin, R. (1989). *Literature through the eyes of faith*. San Francisco: HarperSanFrancisco.

Hadot, P. (1995). *Philosophy as a way of life* (M. Chase, Trans.). Malden, MA: Blackwell.

Handelman, S. (2002). "Stopping the heart": The spiritual search of students and the challenge to a professor in an undergraduate literature class. In A. Sterk (Ed.), *Religion, scholarship, and higher education: Perspectives, models, and future prospects* (pp. 202-230). Notre Dame, IN: University of Notre Dame.

Howard, R. M. (2001). Collaborative pedagogy. In G. Tate, A. Rupiper & K. Schick (Eds.), *A guide to composition pedagogies* (pp. 54-70). New York: Oxford University Press.

Jacobs, A. (2001). Bakhtin and the hermeneutics of love. In S. M. Felch & P. J. Contino (Eds.), *Bakhtin and religion: A feeling for faith* (pp. 25-47). Evanston, IL: Northwestern University Press.

Jeffrey, D. L. (1996). *People of the book: Christian identity and literary culture*. Grand Rapids, MI: William B. Eerdmans.

Lunsford, A. Collaboration, control, and the idea of a writing center. In R. W. Barnett & J. S. Blumner (Eds.), *The Allyn and Bacon guide to writing center theory and practice* (pp. 79-91). Boston: Allyn and Bacon.

McGrath, A. (Ed.). (2001) *Christian literature: An anthology*. Malden, MA: Blackwell.

McKenna, D. L. (2001). *How to read a Christian book*. Grand Rapids, MI: Baker Books.

Morrison, K. F. (1992). *Conversion and text: The cases of Augustine of Hippo, Herman-Judah, and Constantine Tsatsos*. Charlottesville: University of Virginia.

Murphy, C. (2001). The Writing center and social constructionist theory. In R.W. Barnett & J. S. Blumner (Eds.), *The Allyn and Bacon guide to writing center theory and practice* (pp. 110-123). Boston: Allyn and Bacon.

Nussbaum, M. C. (1990). *Love's knowledge: Essays on philosophy and literature*. New York: Oxford University Press.

Ryken, L. (1989). *The liberated imagination: Thinking Christianly about the arts*. Colorado Springs, CO: Waterbrook Press.

Soskice, J. M. (2002). Monica's tears: Augustine on words and speech. *New Blackfriars, 83*(980), 448-458.

Stock, B. (1998). *Augustine the reader: Meditation, self-knowledge, and the ethics of interpretation*. Cambridge, MA: The Belknap Press of Harvard University Press.

Stock, B. (2001). *After Augustine: The meditative reader and the text*. Philadelphia: University of Pennsylvania.

Voiku, D. J. (1997). *A primer on the language theory of St. Augustine.* Lewiston, NY: The Edwin Mellen Press.

JE&CB 11:2 (2007) 53-66   1366-5456

David I. Smith

Misreading Through the Eyes of Faith: Christian Students' Reading Strategies as Interlanguage

THIS ARTICLE EXPLORES some instances of students offering eccentric interpretations of literary texts under the apparent influence of elements of their Christian assumptions and identities. It suggests that rather than viewing such incidents in terms of either error or self-expression, it might be more fruitful to regard them as representing a kind of interpretive interlanguage (a concept current in applied linguistics) that draws imperfectly upon more developed models of Christian interpretation. Four such models are identified and related to students' interpretive practices.

This paper is concerned with the ways in which Christian students read and misread texts in classrooms, and how this relates to pedagogical approaches to student learning, Christian approaches to interpretation, and formation in the life of faith. My focus will on literary texts, but at least some of the points at issue have analogies in student encounters with other kinds of texts elsewhere in the curriculum. I will seek to relate some examples of student interactions with texts to models of interpretation that can be found in literature on faith and learning. I am interested in the ways in which interpretive moves made more or less naively by Christian students might reflect in embryonic form some of the moves made more polysyllabically by Christian theologians and philosophers. This account is therefore located somewhere between general, principled discussions of how we *ought* to interpret, from which students are commonly absent except in the occasional role of philistines at the gates, and explorations of reader responses that emphasize the validity of the individual construction of meaning.

I will approach these matters through narratives of reading events drawn from my own classes at Calvin College, a Christian liberal arts college belonging to the Christian Reformed Church. Almost all students at the college identify themselves as Christians, most coming from Reformed and evangelical denominations. Throughout the curriculum, students are encouraged to relate their faith to their studies. Students are therefore somewhat primed, at least in a general way, for reading with theological schemata in mind.

The fanatical orchestra: Allegorical and Perspectival Reading

The first incident occurred in a second-year German language class. I had assigned a number of poems by Austrian poet Ernst Jandl to small groups of students. Each group was to read a poem and prepare a presentation, which was to include an oral performance of the poem, reading through the poem with the class to check comprehension, and offering a brief commentary. The goal was to practice reading and talking about short literary texts in German.

One group had Jandl's poem *das fanatische orchester* ("the fanatical orchestra") (Jandl, 1981), which describes in a series of increasingly bizarre couplets the breakdown of communication between a conductor and an orchestra apparently determined to misinterpret his every gesture in the most literally-minded way possible. At the outset, the conductor raises his baton, and the players promptly swing their instruments into the air. The conductor opens his lips, and the players start howling. When he taps on the lectern, they smash their instruments, and when he spreads his arms, they begin fluttering around the room. He lowers his head and they begin to dig their way into the floor. Sweat breaks out on the conductor's forehead, and in response the players act as if they are fighting a flood. He raises his eyes, and they "rush toward heaven." Finally, he "stands aflame," perhaps mortified with embarrassment, while the players "collapse in an ardent blaze."

The poem seemed to me to raise in memorable and quirky fashion the point that communicative gestures depend on certain kinds of consensus within ordered domains of language use for their meaning – if we refuse to play by the communally established rules of the game then meaning becomes radically unstable. The orchestra's actions are absurd but not arbitrary; the correspondence is simply not the communally accepted one. Thinking that we might enjoy the humor and then reflect briefly together on the conventional nature of language and communication, I was unprepared when the group of three students assigned this poem proceeded to present it as a detailed allegory of the crucifixion of Christ.

In their reading, the conductor's raising of his baton became the lifting up of the Son of Man on the cross, the orchestra's chaotic response became the rebellion of the jeering crowd, the tapping of the baton became the driving in of the nails, and so on through to the yielding of Christ's spirit and the descent into the fires of Hades. At every point they paired the details of the poem with elements in the crucifixion narratives. It would be an understatement to say that such an approach had not occurred to me, and my immediate inward response was incredulity (of, I must admit, a rather condescending kind). My impression was that my students were somewhat crudely and immaturely trying to Christianize the poem by forcing an allegorical reading upon it, engaging in a form of Christian voice that Chris Anderson describes as "foolishness that is unaware of itself" (Anderson, 1989, p. 12; see also Smart, 2005).

I still think that their reading was at various points forced and mistaken. But when I reread the poem later in the light of their comments, and of other Jandl poems that use crucifixion imagery, I came to the conclusion that they were at least partially right. At the heart of the poem is an image of Christ on the cross, arms outstretched, head bent:

> the conductor spreads out his arms …
> the conductor lowers his head (Jandl, 1981, p. 60)

The orchestra is not, I suggest, the jeering crowds at Golgotha, venting hatred toward the conductor, but rather those who would be his followers. They are, after all, the "fanatical orchestra" – the poem's title seems to suggest not wild rebellion but rather an extreme form of obedience. Every slight gesture of the conductor is paired with an outburst of zealously literalistic mimicry – so zealous that frantic activity accompanies gestures which normally call for heightened still-ness and attentiveness before the beginning of a performance. The problem is not a lack of willingness to obey, but rather transgression of the conventions govern-ing expected responses. What my students rightly identified was an echo of the crucified Christ in the conductor, toward whom the pseudo-obedience is directed. Out of zeal to obey, the poem hints, Christians may also end up engaging in bizarrely inappropriate actions and developing group norms that are increasingly out of touch with the desires of their patient but exasperated Conductor. Where my students erred, I think, was in their identification of the target of the poem's critique and in their overextension of allegorical detail. Where I erred was in fail-ing to see until later the elements of success in their reading.

The results were imperfect, but the strategy is far from new. It exhibits obvious resemblances to the well-known patristic tactic of "despoil[ing] ... literary Egyp-tians of their precious gold" (Jacobs, 2001b, p. 12), in other words allegorizing pagan texts to give them meanings that might be edifying to Christian readers. As Alan Jacobs summarizes in his recent book on the theology of reading,

> Jerome uses an allegorical interpretation of a passage from Scripture
> – the disturbing provision in Deuteronomy (21:10-13) that a woman
> taken captive in warfare may be ritually purified, shaved, and washed,
> and then taken as a wife – to explain how pagan literature may be
> made worthy of Christian use. But it was also common to employ
> allegorical interpretation of the pagan texts themselves in order to ex-
> tract Christian meanings from them, as when Clement of Alexandria
> explicates the scene in the Odyssey in which Odysseus escapes the
> song of the Sirens, who are figured here as sin and error: "Sail past
> their music and leave it behind you, for it will bring about your death.
> But if you will, you can be the victor over the powers of destruction.
> Tied to the wood [of the cross], you shall be freed from destruction."
> (Jacobs, 2001b, pp. 12-13; see also Thistleton, 1992)

On this view, when Christian meanings are assigned to the details of pagan texts (such as Odysseus tied to the mast of his ship), those texts are purified for Christian use. In like manner, my students took a text that appeared to be about an orchestra and made of it an allegory of Christ's passion, thereby bringing it safely within the bounds of Christian discourse. Perhaps Jerome, had he been their German teacher, would have applauded.

Two factors complicate the parallel. First, while the students did work to over-come the surface meanings of the poem, I suspect that they assumed the text to be an allegorical text intended as such by a Christian author – and that assump-tion may have been in a complex sense appropriate, given Jandl's complicated relationship to his Catholic identity. Second, their allegorical strategy led them to hit upon an image that is textually present in the poem in a sense in which the cross of Christ was not present in the text from Homer. If, however, as Gerald Bruns (1992, p. 85) suggests, "allegory is, crudely, the squaring of an alien conceptual scheme with one's own on the charitable assumption that there is a sense (which it is the task of the interpretation to determine) in which they are coherent with one another," then the students' approach was clearly allegorical in both genre and spirit.

Another frame for making sense of the students' reading of the poem is provided by more recent Christian discussions of interpretation in which the aim is not to appropriate texts allegorically as illustrations of Christian theology, but rather to weigh the meaning of the text against the backdrop of one's Christian convictions in order to produce a perspectivally evaluative interpretation. A well-developed example is Nicholas Wolterstorff's theory of the relationship between belief and theory formation (Sloane, 2004). Of course, there are various other models of the perspectival element in interpretation, and other conceptual languages focused on terms such as worldviews, presuppositions, foundational assumptions, tacit knowledge, and so on. Wolterstorff's model will suffice for present purposes, however. Wolterstorff argues that in addition to data beliefs (such as the belief that a certain word recurs several times in the poem and signifies one who conducts an orchestra) and data background beliefs (that is, beliefs that enable one to trust data, such as the belief that my perceptual apparatus is functioning correctly when I look at the printed page), we bring to the act of interpreting the world certain prior hunches and convictions that Wolterstorff terms control beliefs. These are normative beliefs that guide our interpretations by focusing our attention in particular ways and causing us to see certain interpretations as more plausible than others, given their fit or lack of fit with our other convictions about reality (Wolterstorff, 1984, 1999). This does not imply that reality is whatever one's beliefs make it; there are things really present to be noticed or absent to thwart our expectations. The point is rather that "our narrative identities lead us to notice things and believe things which otherwise would almost certainly go unnoticed or unbelieved" (Wolterstorff, 1997b, p. 92). A particular narrative identity, such as that provided by Christian commitment, might position us to better perceive certain aspects of what is really there, conferring a form of "privileged cognitive access" (Wolterstorff, 1997b). This does not mean that no one else could ever see what the Christian notices, or that the Christian will be unfailingly perceptive, or even that the Christian might not be less likely to perceive some things; it merely suggests that it becomes more likely, all other things being equal, that certain things will be noticed and believed by readers who bring Christian expectations to bear in their reading. Given the profound influence of Christian ideas and texts on Western literature, we might surmise that opportunities for this kind of noticing and believing will be reasonably common in the literature classroom.

Despite the important differences between these two modes of Christian reading, I suggest that my students' reading may have been a combination of the two processes. Either an allegorical approach to the text placed them in a position from which the Christological image became visible, or the noticing of the cruciform posture because of prior sensitization to Christian imagery triggered the broader allegorical reading. Despite the unrefined nature of the results, they were engaged in a form, perhaps more than one form, of Christian reading. That being so, the most fruitful pedagogical response for the Christian educator might be neither to simply correct a misreading figured as error (although the reading was imperfect) nor to simply celebrate their personal interpretation of the poem (although the reading may have been edifying), but to look for ways of helping them to consider and refine their own faith-informed reading strategies.

Such refinement may involve more than fine-tuning the particular strategies adopted, for at least two aspects of their approach are troubling. First, their Christian presuppositions, or narrative identities, and/or their allegorical proclivities led them not only to valid insight but also to over-interpretation and misrepresentation of the text – a common and longstanding critique of allegorical interpretation. As Jacobs comments, Jerome's allusion to the cleansing of the captive woman who is shaved, washed, and purified to make her fit for marital appropriation is a disturbing one. It pictures reading as an act of masculine aggression, imagining the text as a prisoner of war; as Jacobs (2001b, p. 13) puts it, "the captured pagan woman is presumably not asked whether she wants to marry." The implication is that such interpretation, at least with any texts that are not works of Christian theology, is basically a form of forced appropriation that may do violence to the text appropriated and reinforce the self's sense of mastery. Second, as they applied their control beliefs to the act of reading and made the text conform to their existing horizons, the students made the text essentially tell them what they already knew about the life of Christ. They bypassed the poem's potential for a more discomfiting questioning of attempts at Christian discipleship, and shielded themselves from being its targets, in the process collapsing the aesthetic distance that, as Pike argues, opens space for spiritual growth (Pike, 2002, 2005). Their manner of reading is in danger of making any new text simply repeat what is already known, thus removing its potential to challenge existing horizons with any force. If Christian reading means imposing an existing Christian schema, then the clear danger is that only comfortable meanings will be allowed to emerge (Wolterstorff, 1997a). I will explore these concerns further in relation to a second reading event.

The true bird: Charitable and Responsive Reading

The second incident, which I have examined at greater length and in a different context (Smith, 2004), took place in the same second-year German language class, although not with the same cohort of students. It involved work with another of Jandl's poems, *der wahre vogel* ("the true bird") (Jandl, 1997). In this poem, the reader is instructed to catch a "dear blackbird," take "tender and fine" scissors, and cut off both of its legs so that it can perpetually fly, higher and higher, until it disappears from view. The persona given voice in the poem tells us that this makes him almost faint with delight, and concludes, "that must be a true bird / that would never think of landing."

This time the reading of the poem was framed differently, the most significant difference being that students were overtly encouraged to engage in a faith-informed reading. After briefly presenting the poem to the class and checking comprehension of vocabulary, I asked them to write in small groups a brief summary of what they would say if asked to deliver a meditation based on this poem at our department's weekly German chapel service. I was surprised at the similarity of most of the responses. Some representative responses went as follows (translated from the German):

> "The theme of the poem is that people are better off once they are freed from earthly limitations."

> "People must be free from everything that holds them down on the ground."

> "'The true bird' by Ernst Jadel [sic] speaks about our freedom in Christ. Christ finds us. He cuts off our legs. Our legs hold us down on the ground of sin. And then we look up and fly higher and higher."

Almost all the students similarly read the poem through a frame in which undesirable earthly limitations are overcome through a spiritual flight of freedom.

There are similarities here to the interpretive moves already described: the poem is read through theologically tinted glasses, it is made into an allegory of salvation, and this leads to questionable interpretive conclusions. Here again, the students' responses are not entirely ungrounded: Jandl's imagery does evoke (if satirically) the escapist soaring that they described, and the line "climbs higher and higher" echoes a couplet from a 19th-century "spiritual poem" by the Romantic poet Joseph von Eichendorff entitled "Durch!" ("Through!"), in which an eagle (the poet's soul) flies higher and higher in search of an opening into heaven, having lost its refuge on earth (Eichendorff, 1975, p. 283). Jandl's calculated appeal to traditional associations of birds and flight with spiritual elevation, and my own framing of the activity as a chapel meditation, along with motifs absorbed from popular Christian media, combined to evoke the students' readings – readers' reactions are typically responsive to pedagogical framing (Rosenblatt, 1978, 1980). Those readings are, however, both theologically and textually questionable. Theologically, the idea that salvation manifests itself as mutilation of created capacities and an escape from earthly reality is, however popular, more Gnostic than Christian. Orthodox Christian theology has resisted such Gnostic tendencies, seeing God's original affirmation of the goodness of creation, the incarnation of Christ as the Word made flesh, and the adoption of such basic, earthy staples as bread and wine at the heart of Christian spirituality as signposts to God's desire to renew creation rather than to do away with it (Pannenberg, 1984; Taylor, 1989; Zizioulas, 1986). Textually, the sing-song rhythm and staccato instructions that open the poem, evoking both children's rhymes and the matter-of-fact efficiency of a cookbook recipe, together with the consequences for the bird of incapacitation and starvation, reveal a tone rather darker than that identified by the students (Schmidt-Dengler, 2001). Jandl parodies a Romantic worldview that associates the poet with other-worldly transcendence and is more critical than affirming of escapist spirituality (his closing line brings the eye firmly down to earth and alludes to a 19th-century German folk song about a journeyman miller, the chorus of which declares, "That must be a poor miller / that would never think of journeying" [Müller, 1818]). As with the orchestra, the poem's critique has been evaded in the students' assimilations of it to their existing theological frames.

On this occasion, my response was more constructive than veiled disbelief. I began to pose questions intended to force closer attention to the tone and implications of the text and suggest other possibilities for making the connection with faith. The relationship between faith and materiality is a recurrent theme in Jandl's poems, making questions such as the following pertinent to Jandl's as well as this class's horizon: Is it normal, natural, or comfortable for a bird to have its legs amputated? Could that be part of God's intentions? Could it be an act of love? What words describe the amputations? Are scissors "tender"? What genres do the style and rhythm bring to mind? Do these accents suggest concern for the bird's well-being? If the amputation were an image of salvation, what would that imply about God? Does God engage in acts of childish cruelty? Is salvation like food preparation? Can we read mutilation as liberation? What future does this bird have? What can it now *not* do? Is perpetual flight freedom, in the absence of eating, resting, mating? How should we hear the protestations of tenderness and joy in the light of all this? Who or what is Jandl's target? Are we, even in our faith, like the persona in the poem, expressing joy at flights of transcendence but rather callously out of touch with created reality? How often do we soar on the wings of Wesley during worship but make inadequate practical connections with life the next morning? Do we too easily end up locked in slogan or mission-statement mode, forever rearticulating to one another our resonant phrases, at times uncomfortably aware of a certain gap between the big picture categories and the daily detail of life, and at times complicit in sustaining this gap because we welcome the scissors and secretly prefer other-worldly inspiration to the more ambiguous challenges of concrete implementation? Does our faith have legs?

This questioning process suggests the possibility of a path of development that, instead of displacing faith in the name of sophistication, moves in the direction of a deeper reading that remains faith-framed. It implicitly invokes two further models of Christian reading. The first focuses on *charitable* reading, on a certain quality of self-giving attentiveness to the text that offers personal vulnerability to the wisdom that can be drawn from it. Such reading approaches any text as a neighbor whom we are called to love (Griffiths, 2002; Jones, 2002) – Christian charity accordingly "demands that we extend the gift of love to all books" (Jacobs, 2001b, p. 32). Mikhail Bakhtin suggests that reading that is not loving will end up either fragmenting a text into its component parts or absorbing it into some preconceived schema or set of pre-established categories, this latter surely being an apt description of what my students did with both Jandl poems (Bakhtin, 1993; Jacobs, 2001a). Instead, the hallmark of charitable reading will be loving attention to the details of the text in order to see it whole in its own integrity. As Bakhtin puts it, "The valued manifoldness of Being as human ... can present itself only to loving contemplation .... Lovelessness, indifference, will never be able to generate sufficient attention to slow down and linger intently over an object, to hold and sculpt every detail and particular in it, however minute" (cited in Jacobs, 2001a, p. 27). This does not mean becoming a blank slate – Bakhtin characterizes such reading as a taking of intentional moral responsibility before the text, not an evacuation of the reader's self – and so this stance qualifies but does not necessarily negate allegorical or perspectival appropriations.[1] What it challenges is the danger of interpretive violence; charity should combine with humility and self-denial to enable a receptivity to meanings in the text that challenge the reader's sense of his or her own goodness (Schwehn, 1993; Spina, 1989; Westphal, 1998).

This already points us to a fourth model of Christian reading, one implicit in the initial choice to ask the students to think about the text in terms of a chapel meditation, a form of public exhortation to the life of faith. In this model, the emphasis is not only upon the love enacted in attentiveness to the text, but on the degree to which responsiveness to the call heard through the text results in living the life of love. Augustine's suggestion that the test of an act of reading is whether it produces increased love of God and neighbor in the reader is perhaps the most influential formulation of this model, in which a moral relationship is established between text and reader and the quality of Christian reading is expressed in the quality of consequent Christian living (Jacobs, 2001a; Smith, 2004). While this relationship is clearest and strongest in relationship to sacred texts, the theological tradition has also commonly been open to the possibility that the voice of wisdom and the call to love may be heard through other texts (e.g., from a literary treatment of human experience to a scientific examination of environmental decay), which may therefore in their own manner demand life response (Griffiths, 2002; Huelin, 2005). There are fresh dangers here of ignoring the fine grain of the text as long as the outcome seems to smell sweet, but the emphasis on response is in principle combinable with our other models of Christian reading. On this view, perhaps our reading of Jandl's text was Christian to the degree that students were indeed challenged to sober self-examination and greater obedience; I will discuss the prospects of that outcome further below.

Interlanguage and Pedagogical Stance

I would like at this point to step back from these accounts of particular reading events to consider what they imply concerning pedagogical stance. I have suggested that the reading processes engaged in by students in these two classrooms can be correlated with a variety of well-developed accounts of faith-informed reading that are represented in the Christian tradition. Specifically, I have suggested that what might broadly be called allegorical, perspectival, charitable, and responsive approaches to the act of reading can be found at work in the classroom events described. Perhaps these are sometimes different phases of the reading experience; perhaps they are appropriate in different ways to different texts; or perhaps we should think of Christian reading in a more integrated way as combining a determination to relate all things to Christ with a sensitivity to differences in worldview, a loving attentiveness to the text and a readiness to hear in any text a potential challenge to more faithful living. There are also doubtless other relevant modes of reading, including simple playful delight in the creational possibilities of language. Whatever we conclude concerning these questions, my interest here is in the partially formed nature of the models employed in the classroom incidents described here.

These incidents suggest that questionable student readings of texts may be neither simply decoding errors to be corrected, nor simply expressions of personal meaning to be celebrated. They may indwell communal systems of faith-informed interpretation of the world (such as an allegorical strategy of textual appropriation) and communally current systems or expressions of theology (such as an escapist theology of salvation). I suggest that attentiveness to these dimensions of students' acts of interpretation could be educationally fruitful, and that the possibility that students' faith-informed misinterpretations might evidence a kind of partially developed "interlanguage" of Christian interpretation should be explored.

The concept of *interlanguage* is drawn from second language acquisition theory. Since the 1960s and 1970s, this concept has changed how linguistic errors committed by second language learners are understood in language learning contexts (Corder, 1967; Doughty & Long, 2003; Selinker, 1972). For earlier behaviorist models, an error was a wrong behavior and potential bad habit to be eradicated as swiftly as possible by direct counterattack (correction, drilling, etc.). Cognitive approaches attended more to the systematicity of learner errors – a non-native learner of English who writes, for instance, "I flied my kite" is showing competence as much as incompetence, for the mistaken form "flied" reflects over-application of a valid rule for forming past tense utterances. Such utterances are manifestations of an interlanguage – an intermediate linguistic system that is neither the mother tongue of the learner nor yet quite the target language being learned, but which has its own patterns and systematicity influenced by both linguistic systems, as well as by other factors such as effects of first language training and adaptive learner strategies for communication while in a state of imperfect mastery. Errors produced in meaningful language use situations now become potential evidence of the state of the learner's interlanguage, and material for reflection on how the teacher can best help that system to move closer to the target language model (the idea that we can just briskly drill it into shape has decreased in plausibility as language acquisition and the role of teacher input have been more closely studied).

The parallel should not be pushed too far – I am concerned here primarily with the mindset with which we approach student interpretive moves rather than with detailed correspondences between hermeneutics and language acquisition. I suggest, however, that it might be helpful to think of something loosely analogous to interlanguage taking place in Christian students' partially formed efforts to master a "grammar" of Christian reading. Although imperfect, this analogy could serve to foster a particular kind of pedagogic attentiveness to learner (mis)readings of texts. Christian students working at interpreting texts in Christian classrooms are pictured as positioned between, on the one hand, reading practices and strategies learned from their general socialization and exposure to texts in various social settings and, on the other hand, those practices representative of responsible (and, in this case, mature Christian) interpretation into which they are (ideally) being socialized in educational settings. Their patterns of response to texts will exhibit, more or less systematically, characteristics of both sources of interpretive strategies, as well as being influenced by other contextual factors such as adaptive strategies for dealing with the task set in relation to the text assigned. Insofar as faith is "'enacted' in discourse and sustained through particular kinds of interpretive practice," the "grammar" of Christian interpretation may at any given point manifest itself in student interpretations as an immature system. If this is the case, then approaching odd student interpretations as simply errors or valid reader responses may miss opportunities for growth (Rand, 2001).

The implication of thinking about clumsy student readings in this way is that the goal of learning, along with the pedagogical strategies chosen to achieve it, needs to be thought about in terms of simultaneous processes of growth in engagement with the text and in sophistication regarding Christian reading strategies. As I have suggested, while the strategies applied by my students were susceptible to professorial critique, they were recognizable as Christian approaches to reading as elaborated in the Christian theological and philosophical tradition. While the focus of learning was in each case a particular literary text, students would also benefit in terms of both intellectual growth and Christian maturity from more self-critical appropriation of these faith-informed reading approaches. The analogy with interlanguage suggests the possible value of attending to apparently crude interpretive moves on the part of students as evidence of underlying interpretive approaches that could be nudged toward more mature forms. This further implies the value of becoming more explicit with students about reading stances and their relationship to faith.

Student Response

This paper has focused on suggestive incidents of faith-informed misreading; adequate documentation of the fruits of the approach advocated (and the applicability or limits of the interlanguage analogy) requires longitudinal empirical study and goes beyond the bounds of this essay. I would like, however, to close with a final sample of student response that indicates significant potential benefits of constructive reflection with students on emerging Christian approaches to interpretation.

Subsequent to the incidents described above, I engaged in a substantial redesign of an upper level survey course in 20th-century German literature. I had become dissatisfied with the ways in which the existing syllabus and assignments encouraged rapid, once-only, consumerist scanning of large blocks of text and implicitly affirmed the assumption that such reading was adequate for arriving at quick interpretive judgments as part of class discussion. While in previous iterations of the course there had been a clear strand of perspectival interpretation, relating themes in the texts studied to Christian beliefs and concerns, I wanted to explore ways of structuring learning that might also foster charitable and responsive approaches to these texts. I cannot describe the changes made in detail here (I intend to do so in a future paper), but they included making space for guided repeat readings of certain texts, adding a regular program of poetry reading, re-reading, and journaling that stretched throughout the semester alongside the more extensive readings, changing assessment tasks, including an assigned period of meditation on a key text, and including on a regular basis brief texts from Christian thinkers about the nature of Christian reading. Short periods of class time were set aside at periodic intervals to discuss the nature of charitable reading and the students' experiences of trying to practice such reading in this and other courses. In these ways, students were encouraged to reflect explicitly on the ways in which their own approaches to reading might reflect wider Christian reflection on interpretation, and the examples from the earlier sections of this paper were shared with students late in the semester. At times there were clear examples both of uncharitable, dismissive readings of texts and of theologically limited understandings of the idea of charitable reading (early in the semester during discussion, several students identified reading charitably with liking or enjoying a text, reflecting an undifferentiated conception of "love").

In final journal entries at the end of the semester, students were asked to reflect on what they had learned about the idea of faith-informed reading. Quoted below are some paragraphs drawn from one of these final journal entries:

> Not long ago, I took reading Christianly and applied it to the way I read people. I noticed myself casting rash judgments on people without understanding them, knowing their backgrounds, or even talking to them. I think especially because of the focus in this class to read Christianly, I tried to change this bad habit. I had an opportunity to practice reading people Christianly only this past weekend. A middle-aged man from out of town came in, in search of a computer. He claimed he had been wandering around Grand Rapids for the past two days in search of his sister, who he only knew lived somewhere near Kentwood. He didn't have her phone number and needed to look it up online (in an email because she was unlisted). Beaners [a local coffee shop] doesn't have computers though, only internet service. My co-worker wanted to get him out; she thought he was off his rocker. But I talked to him for a little while, and upon hearing he hadn't eaten in at least a day, gave him a sandwich and a cup of coffee, and told him he could ask one of our customers to use their computer. One gentleman was kind enough to let him. So he got on, and couldn't find her number, but left a message for her to come and pick him up, he would be waiting.
>
> Having been in a similar situation once myself (lost in Germany), I was sensitive to his needs and feeling of exhaustion and helplessness. I took my own experience and related it to his, and because of my Christianity, I asked myself over and over what the right thing to do would be. Like skimming over a text leave[s] one unsatisfied, and does an injustice to text and author, I was not at peace having briefly met this man, to leave him out on Breton for the night. I had to go back (with a male friend), if only to keep him company for a short while, but possibly to bring him somewhere to spend the night.

In this way, I believe, allowing time to get to know a work (or person), realizing from what sort of framework we're looking at it, and doing so lovingly, this is how we should read Christianly.[2]

In this journal entry, the student responds explicitly to the focus on Christian interpretation that had run through the semester, and indicates awareness of development – the opening "not long ago" refers back to a journal entry a couple of weeks earlier in which the student had begun to reflect on wider applications of charitable reading outside the classroom as a result of an experience of misreading a stranger based on quick judgments. Changes in perception and behavior are related directly to the focus of the class ("because of the focus in this class to read Christianly"), and there is an unprompted extension of these themes to other experiences ("reading people Christianly"). The student shows explicit awareness of the role (and dangers) of prior identity and interpretive frameworks ("she thought he was off his rocker"; "having been in a similar situation once myself"; "realizing from what sort of framework we're looking at it"). She also offers striking evidence of applying the focus on charitable reading responsively to concrete Christian living and growth in Christian maturity.

The first incident discussed in this paper showed students applying immature versions of recognizably Christian reading strategies. The second showed similar processes at work, and also traced a classroom movement from the initial strategies adopted by learners to a more robust but still faith-informed reading. I have argued that student interpretations such as those described should be approached in the spirit in which applied linguists have studied interlanguage – neither simply rejected as error nor simply affirmed because of its status as personal reader response, but rather taken as a stage in a maturation process that can be pedagogically assisted toward complex but describable goals. I suggest that this last example, a journal entry describing a growing understanding and application of the idea of Christian reading, indicates that a constructive focus on students' growth in faith-informed reading practices can yield significant benefits.

Notes

1   On a possible relationship between allegory and charity, see the definition of allegory from Bruns quoted above, which describes allegory as grounded in a charitable assumption that texts have meaning in relation to already understood truths. The question of whether allegory is inherently violent to the text depends somewhat on the theory of textual meaning that is assumed; see, e.g., Huelin, 2005. Bruns argues that Augustine combined an openness to allegorical reading with an emphasis on the conversion of the reader by the text, such that reading "implies a process in which one reinterprets oneself in order to enter into the conceptual scheme of another" (1992, p. 143).

2   Student journal, German 308: Twentieth-Century German Literature II, Calvin College, May 2006, quoted with permission.

Bibliography

Anderson, C. (1989). The description of an embarrassment: When students write about religion. *ADE Bulletin, 94*, 12.

Bakhtin, M. M. (1993). *Toward a philosophy of the act* (V. Liapunov, Trans.). Austin, TX: University of Texas Press.

Bruns, G. L. (1992). *Hermeneutics ancient and modern.* New Haven, CT: Yale University Press.

Corder, S. P. (1967). The significance of learners' errors. *International Review of Applied Linguistics, 5*, 161-170.

Doughty, C. J., & Long, M. H. (2003). *The handbook of second language acquisition.* Oxford: Blackwell.

Eichendorff, J. v. (1975). *Sämtliche Gedichte.* München: Deutscher Taschenbuch Verlag.

Griffiths, P. J. (2002). Reading as a spiritual practice. In L. G. Jones & S. Paulsell (Eds.), *The scope of our art: The vocation of the theological teacher* (pp. 32-47). Grand Rapids, MI: Eerdmans.

Huelin, S. (2005). Toward a theological ontology of textual meaning. *Christian Scholar's Review, 34*(2), 217-233.

Jacobs, A. (2001a). Bakhtin and the hermeneutics of love. In S. M. Felch & P. J. Contino (Eds.), *Bakhtin and religion: A feeling for faith* (pp. 25-45). Evanston, IL: Northwestern University Press.

Jacobs, A. (2001b). *A theology of reading: The hermeneutics of love.* Boulder, CO: Westview Press.

Jandl, E. (1981). *die bearbeitung der mütze.* Darmstadt: Luchterhand.

Jandl, E. (1997). *Poetische Werke 8: der gelbe hund / selbstporträt des schachspielers als trinkende uhr.* München: Luchterhand.

Jones, L. G. (2002). Formed and transformed by scripture: Character, community, and authority in biblical interpretation. In W. P. Brown (Ed.), *Character and scripture: Moral formation, community and biblical tradition* (pp. 18-33). Grand Rapids, MI: Eerdmans.

Müller, W. (1818). Das Wandern ist des Müllers Lust. Available online at http://ingeb. org/Lieder/DasWande.html (accessed 15 December 2003).

Pannenberg, W. (1984). *Christian spirituality and sacramental community.* London: Darton, Longman and Todd.

Pike, M. A. (2002). Aesthetic distance and the spiritual journey: Educating for spiritually and morally significant experiences across the art and literature curriculum. *International Journal of Children's Spirituality, 7*(1), 9-21.

Pike, M. A. (2005). Reading and responding to biblical texts: Aesthetic distance and the spiritual journey. In C. Ota & C. Erricker (Eds.), *Spiritual education: Literary, empirical and pedagogical approaches* (pp. 189-201). Brighton: Sussex Academic Press.

Rand, L. (2001). Enacting faith: Evangelical discourse and the discipline of composition studies. *College Composition and Communication, 52*(3), 349-367.

Rosenblatt, L. M. (1978). *The Reader, the text, the poem: The transactional theory of the literary work.* Carbondale: Southern Illinois University Press.

Rosenblatt, L. M. (1980). "What facts does this poem teach you?" *Language Arts,* 57(4), 386-394.

Schmidt-Dengler, W. (2001). *Der wahre Vogel: Sechs Studien zum Gedenken an Ernst Jandl.* Wien: Edition Praesens.

Schwehn, M. (1993). *Exiles from Eden: Religion and the academic vocation in America.* New York: Oxford University Press.

Selinker, L. (1972). Interlanguage. *International Review of Applied Linguistics, 10*, 209-231.

Sloane, A. (2004). *On being a Christian in the academy: Nicholas Wolterstorff and the practice of Christian scholarship.* Carlisle: Paternoster Press.

Smart, J. M. (2005). "Frankenstein or Jesus Christ?" When the voice of faith creates a monster for the composition teacher. In E. Vander Lei & B. L. Kyburz (Eds.), *Negotiating religious faith in the composition classroom* (pp. 11-23). Portsmouth, NH: Heinemann.

Smith, D. I. (2004). The poet, the child and the blackbird: aesthetic reading and spiritual development. *International Journal of Children's Spirituality, 9*(2), 143-154.

Spina, F. A. (1989). Revelation, reformation, re-creation: Canon and the theological foundation of the Christian university. *Christian Scholar's Review, 18*(4), 315-332.

Taylor, C. (1989). *Sources of the self: The making of the modern identity.* Cambridge, MA: Harvard University Press.

Thistleton, A. C. (1992). *New horizons in hermeneutics: The theory and practice of transforming Bible reading.* London: HarperCollins.

Westphal, M. (1998). *Suspicion and faith: The religious uses of modern atheism.* New York: Fordham University Press.

Wolterstorff, N. (1984). *Reason within the bounds of religion* (2nd ed.). Grand Rapids, MI: Eerdmans.

Wolterstorff, N. (1997a). The importance of hermeneutics for a Christian worldview. In R. Lundin (Ed.), *Disciplining hermeneutics: Interpretation in Christian perspective* (pp. 25-47). Grand Rapids, MI: Eerdmans.

Wolterstorff, N. (1997b). Suffering, power, and privileged cognitive access: The revenge of the particular. In D. A. Hoekema & B. Fong (Eds.), *Christianity and culture in the crossfire* (pp. 79-94). Grand Rapids, MI: Eerdmans.

Wolterstorff, N. (1999). Can scholarship and Christian conviction mix? A new look at the integration of knowledge. *Journal of Education and Christian Belief, 3*(1), 33-49.

Zizioulas, J. D. (1986). The early Christian community. In B. McGinn & J. Meyendorff (Eds.), *Christian spirituality: origins to the twelfth century* (Vol. 16, pp. 23-43). London: Routledge & Kegan Paul.

JE&CB 11:2 (2007) 67-82   1366-5456

John Netland

"Who Is My Neighbor?" Reading World Literature Through the Hermeneutics of Love

WORLD LITERATURE COURSES *reflect both the academy's and the Christian community's interest in a global education, but what theoretical assumptions inform the teaching of world literature? The oft-cited rationale for cultural diversity may prove insufficient if it leads merely to the assertion of difference as a self-justifying good. This essay claims a richer model of diversity, drawing on biblical themes as well as recent definitions of world literature and cosmopolitanism, to open up a hermeneutical space for transcultural understanding. The essay also argues that the study of world literature in the Christian classroom should be informed by a hermeneutic of charity which directs our reading toward love of God and neighbor.*

Over the past fifteen years, the college where I teach has sought to make its curriculum more international and multicultural, encouraging off-campus and overseas experiences, developing service-learning and social justice initiatives, and offering new degree programs with international emphases. Such initiatives match trends in the academy, which are often justified on pragmatic grounds such as preparing our students for an increasingly globalized work force. Our reasons extend beyond the pragmatic, for we see these global initiatives as an expression of our service to a multicultural kingdom of God (Calvin College, 2004, p. 9). My contribution to these initiatives has been to teach world literature. The course is popular with our students, many of whom arrive on campus with first-hand experience of another culture and a curiosity to learn more about the cultural plenitude of our world. Nor do these students need to be persuaded of the values of diversity and tolerance. However, I am finding that theorizing the class through the constructs of diversity and tolerance can leave us at times with little more to say than expressing appreciative and non-judgmental observations about the cultures we encounter through literature. Do such sentiments short-circuit our obligations as critical thinkers and as a reading community committed to the ethics of God's kingdom? What difference would it make if, rather than making diversity the primary focus of our reading, we frame the world literature classroom in a hermeneutic of love?

Diversity is seldom defined with any precision, but it often seems to stand as a synonym for "difference." Granted, diversity can mean difference, but it can also imply plenitude and multiplicity as well. Such meanings are implicit in David I. Smith and Barbara Carvill's reading of the Genesis creation account, from which they conclude that "Spreading, creativity, diversity – all are rooted in creation prior to the fall" (Smith and Carvill, 2000, p. 6; emphasis in the original). Diversity in this context emphasizes the variegated profusion of life in addition to its different manifestations. That distinction may seem minor, but it suggests that the variety rooted in creation does not emphasize the mutually exclusive nature of differences as much as it does their complementary variety and abundance. Such diversity in the created order functions less for the purpose of asserting the differences between species than of appreciating the incredible richness and complexity of creation. Significantly, diversity in the biblical accounts is apparent both in the origins and the ends of the Christian story; both the creation account of Genesis and the Apocalypse's vision of the people of God drawn "from every tribe and language and people and nation" (Rev 5:9) reflect a variety and plenitude that derive their worth from the God who created and redeems this world.

Conventional references to diversity have little to do with that theological context but instead are almost always accompanied by exhortations to celebrate our differences, a sentiment that in the United States may owe as much to the myth of American individualism as it does to multicultural theory. In my world literature classrooms, I have often heard such affirmations of diversity in ways that imply difference to be, if not an end in itself, at least the irrevocable condition of our humanity. This way of thinking about diversity, I would argue, parallels a pervasive misreading of Edward Said's critique of "Eurocentrism" in his ground-breaking book *Orientalism* and offers a dubious theoretical framework for teaching world literature.

It has been nearly 30 years since Said chastened the Western academy for its construction of such essentialized concepts as "the Orient" or "Oriental." *Orientalism* reminded us that we read, experience, and interpret reality as culturally contingent humans, and Said challenged what he called "Eurocentric" ways of thinking. But if our ways of knowing are inevitably culturally inscribed, does this not question the possibility of reaching across the cultural divide that separates us from other cultures and other perspectives? Can we move beyond our ethnocentrism to a genuine understanding of the other? Said certainly believed that such rapprochement was possible, and he was distressed in later years to see how his deconstruction of Eurocentrism seemed to have inspired a variety of "other"-centrisms, like Islamocentric or Afrocentric theories of knowledge (Said, 1994, p. 150). Said criticized these counter-discourses as "identity politics" that actually trade on the "epistemology of imperialism." That epistemology, Said argues, "is the supremely stubborn thesis that everyone is principally and irreducibly a member of some race or category, and that race or category cannot ever be assimilated to or accepted by others – except as itself" (Said, 1994, p. 148). Such misreadings of Said to give sanction to the notion that we are irreducibly identified by race, gender, class, ethnicity, culture, or nationality can sometimes make assertions of diversity lead to the dead-end game that, according to Kwame Anthony Appiah, ultimately leaves us unable to converse. All we can say, asserts Appiah (2006), is that

> "From where I stand, I am right. From where you stand, you are right." And there would be nothing further to say. From our different perspectives, we would be living effectively in different worlds. And

without a shared world, what is there to discuss? People often recommend relativism because they think it will lead to tolerance. But if we cannot learn from one another what it is right to think and feel and do, then conversation between us will be pointless. Relativism of that sort isn't a way to encourage conversation; it's just a reason to fall silent. (pp. 30-31)

Such silences occasionally intrude into our classroom discussions when well-meaning students find themselves caught between their own ethical judgment and their reticence to impose their own values onto others. Such stances may seem principled, but they can also make it very easy to ignore human suffering and injustice in other societies as unfortunate realities that are ultimately not our concern. Rather than allowing my students to settle into this easy tolerance, I want them to engage more deeply with other peoples and cultures, to see themselves as agents of reconciliation in a world where difference is often less a source of celebration than a justification for oppression.

Re-Conceiving the Hermeneutical Situation of the World Literature Classroom

To reach that deeper level of engagement, we need a hermeneutical model that admits the possibility of achieving interpretive understanding, or what Hans-Georg Gadamer (1989) has memorably phrased the "fusion of ... horizons," wherein the reader's interpretive horizon and that of the text meet (p. 306). There must be some possibility that we as readers can reach across the interpretive divide to understand the text and its cultural and historical horizons. Rather than situating the world literature classroom in the hermeneutics of difference, I would like to explore an alternative hermeneutical model. As readers, my students and I inhabit a particular temporal and cultural horizon, and the literary texts mediate between us and their originating horizons. While understanding the text is an important hermeneutical objective, I am also drawn to ethical models of reading, like Alan Jacobs's notion of hermeneutical charity, which situates reading practices within the context of Jesus' summary of the greatest commandments – to love God and neighbor. Similarly, Smith's and Carvill's invocation of the "gift of the stranger" (2000) suggests a model of cross-cultural hospitality that informs their foreign language pedagogy but also can illuminate our cross-cultural reading practices.

Jacobs (2001) suggests that the Christian reader might need to subordinate a correct interpretation of a text – long presumed to be the primary objective of reading – to the law of love. Referring both to Jesus' summary of the law as loving God and loving neighbor and to Augustine's belief that an interpretation of Scripture which advances charity – regardless of authorial intent – is a good interpretation, Jacobs argues that a charitable reading "requires that books and authors, however alien to the beliefs and practices of the Christian life, be understood and treated as neighbors" (p. 13). Moreover, reading practices should be "directed toward God and neighbor ... (*caritas*)" rather than "directed toward the self ... (*cupiditas*)" (p. 31). Lest such a hermeneutic of love be misconstrued as an "intolerably mushy ... sentimentality," Jacobs reminds us that love is made of much sterner stuff than sentimentality and the unreflexive non-judgmentalism that passes too often for tolerance. Rather, Jacobs seeks to show "how a genuinely Christian notion of love requires among other things a deep commitment to discriminating judgment" (p. 14).

Smith and Carvill (2000) make a case that a biblical model of hospitality should shape their pedagogy of second language acquisition. Building on a reading of creation that affirms diversity to be a distinctive feature of the creational order and therefore a reflection of creational goodness rather than a result of the fall, Smith and Carvill also recognize that the differences (including languages) which separate peoples, cultures, and nations often expose underlying conflicts and injustices. As such, they appeal to "a biblical vision for reconciliation, for justice and peace among nations. It must be shaped by respect for the other as an image bearer of God; it must be eager to hear the other; and it must be driven by love for God and for one's neighbor" (p. 57). This love for one's neighbor leads to a form of hospitality that, as the titular "gift of the stranger" implies, represents the blessing both to the host and to the stranger (pp. 101-102). Their attention to the ways in which travel comprises a primary means of cultural change (see especially pp. 115-117) has a particular resonance to the world literature classroom, for – as my subsequent reading of John Keats will show – our reading of world literature is itself a form of vicarious travel, and we need to consider how our imaginative travel can take us beyond the literary tourism that reduces the other to an exotic object or to a self-referential mirror.

The hermeneutic of *caritas* that I infer from Jacobs and Smith and Carvill emphasizes the following features: reading world literature and understanding that its varied cultural horizons are in some sense related to the biblical vision of reconciliation and renewal. We confess a faith in God's redemptive purposes for a world that still bears the marks of its created goodness and beauty but is also tainted by a pervasive brokenness, a condition that characterizes cultures as well as people. We read about other people and cultures as part of our own participation in God's redemptive purposes, learning to love the people and cultures we encounter through the text, learning what it means to love them as our neighbor. Such a purpose demands that we approach the text with a generosity of spirit and a willingness to engage in authentic dialogue. It does not demand that we jettison moral judgment altogether in the mistaken notion that tolerance means the tacit approval of all customs in the name of cultural difference. Rather, our moral judgment should be shaped by the ethics of Christ's kingdom and the humility that acknowledges our shared human finitude.

While the hermeneutic of *caritas* clarifies the purposes of our reading, we still need a hermeneutical model that can help us bridge the interpretive gap that separates us from the text's cultural horizons. In referring to David Damrosch's theorizing of the doubleness of world literature and Appiah's notion of "cosmopolitanism," I am seeking conceptual models that define diversity through a pluralistic logic of multiple identities rather than the zero-sum game of binary oppositions. Damrosch (2003) describes "world literature" as literature that has a dual identity – both as a product of its particular cultural and linguistic origin and as "literary works that circulate beyond their culture of origin, either in translation or in their original language" (p. 4). He states that "works become world literature by being received *into* the space of a foreign culture" but that the space the work then inhabits becomes "the locus of a negotiation between two different cultures." Damrosch describes this negotiation as "a double refraction, one that can be described through the figure of the ellipse, with the source and host cultures providing the two foci that generate the elliptical space within which a work lives as world literature, connected to both cultures, circumscribed by neither alone" (p. 283). Damrosch's "elliptical space" can define the world literature classroom: as readers, we form a "host community," defined by our particular reading and cultural practices. Our literary texts emerge from a variety of "national"[1] contexts, and the classroom brings these texts to life in a dialogue (what Damrosch calls a double refraction) between ourselves and the worlds of the texts.

While Damrosch's image of the ellipse focuses primarily on the literary text, Appiah's notion of cosmopolitanism theorizes how we as humans can maintain multiple identities as both citizens of the cosmos and residents of particularized, local communities. Appiah speaks of "two ideals – universal concern and respect for legitimate difference" as intertwining strands of cosmopolitanism: "One is the idea that we have obligations to others, obligations that stretch beyond those to whom we are related by the ties of kith and kind, or even the more formal ties of a shared citizenship. The other is that we take seriously the value not just of human life but of particular human lives, which means taking an interest in the practices and beliefs that lend them significance" (Appiah, 2006, p. xv). Thus, we have obligations not only toward those with whom we share natural affinities but also with a broader human community, a sentiment not unlike Jesus' explication of the command to love one's neighbor, which in Luke's account leads into the parable of the Good Samaritan (Luke 10:25-37). Our neighbor, as it turns out, might be quite unlike us, and yet somehow in the presence of that difference lies the possibility of meaningful exchange and mutual obligation.

Beyond Literary Tourism

My world literature class begins with a unit on quest or journey narratives. We read from Thomas Foster's engaging book *How to Read Literature Like a Professor* and evaluate his claim that "the real reason for a quest is always self-knowledge" (Foster, 2003, p. 3). While we find ample support for his contention, in the course of writing this essay I have been wondering if that claim might reveal an incipient narcissism in literary journeys and quests. To raise such questions, I intend now to open the first day of class with Keats's sonnet "On First Looking into Chapman's Homer." This poem has been a delight to teach in my British literature survey, both because the poem so perfectly embodies the Petrarchan sonnet and because its figuration of reading as voyages of discovery attests to a nearly universal experience among avid readers. Like Keats, we travel vicariously through literature, finding similar pleasures in the discovery of "goodly states and kingdoms":

> Much have I traveled in the realms of gold,
>   And many goodly states and kingdoms seen;
>   Round many western islands have I been

Which bards in fealty to Apollo hold.
Oft of one wide expanse had I been told
    That deep-browed Homer ruled as his demesne;
    Yet did I never breathe its pure serene
Till I heard Chapman speak out loud and bold:
Then felt I like some watcher of the skies
    When a new planet swims into his ken;
Or like stout Cortez when with eagle eyes
    He stared at the Pacific – and all his men
Looked at each other with a wild surmise -
    Silent, upon a peak in Darien.
(Stillinger & Lynch, 2006, pp. 880-81)

In the sestet, where the speaker searches for the right analogy with which to capture his emotional response to this new world, we are given two possibilities: an astronomer who discovers a new planet, and Cortez's first glimpse of the Pacific Ocean. It is the latter image that lingers through the last four lines of the poem, leaving us with the image of the European conquistadors and their discovery (or is it conquest?) of the New World.

What has given this poem some notoriety of the "embarrassing factual blunders great poets make" variety is the substitution of Cortez for Balboa in line 11. Actually, many critics argue that this substitution was not a blunder but a deliberate replacement.[2] The editors of the *Longman Anthology of English Literature* apparently believe this to have been deliberate,[3] while the editors of the *Norton Anthology of English Literature* minimize the mistake with the comment that "none of Keats's contemporaries noticed the error" (Stillinger & Lynch, 2006, p. 880). An earlier edition merely trivializes it: "That it was Balboa, not Cortez, who caught his first sight of the Pacific from the heights of Darien, in Panama, matters to history but not to poetry" (Abrams, 1993, p. 769). I suggest that we encourage our students to wrestle with this question and with its subsequent implications about the relationship of poetry to history and about our reading practices. Does it matter that Keats used the wrong name to represent the first European to set eyes on the Pacific Ocean? Posing this question can take the class from practical criticism (close-reading techniques) to theory (articulating a rationale for why this error matters or not) and then to a comparative discussion about the degree to which our reading practices might be culturally contingent.

When I teach this poem in British literature, few students seem disturbed by this error, perhaps at most enjoying a chuckle at the expense of day-dreaming poets who can't be bothered to check their facts. As I use this poem in world literature, I intend to push my students further to articulate a theory as to why it should or shouldn't matter. My hunch is that those students who find the error inconsequential are likely to explain their view by distinguishing between aesthetic and historiographical concerns, perhaps even echoing modernist claims to a self-enclosed aesthetic realm untainted by the quotidian realities of historical experience. And while many of our classroom practices still trade on at least some kind of distinction between literary and historical categories, it is worth pointing out to our students that many cultures may theorize the relationship between

72

literature and history differently than do modern, Western aesthetics.

Beyond the theoretical question about art and history, I want my students to consider how the allusion to Cortez/Balboa functions in the poem. Does that allusion tell us anything about the historical reality of the conquistadors and their conquests, or does it serve primarily as a marker of the speaker's emotional experience? Here we might want to ask our students how a reader from present-day Central America might read this trope. I was unable to find any reception histories of how this poem has been read in Central America, so my comments here are necessarily speculative. Still, even asking such questions requires us to consider the perspectives of others and what interpretive histories they may bring to the poem. Would such readers find the confusion of Balboa with Cortez innocuous? Teachers who may wish to devote additional time to teasing out such questions could assign students to present background reports on the respective reputations of these two explorers. That the name Balboa graces the currency as well as scores of place names in present-day Panama, while the name of Cortez is notably absent in present-day Mexico speaks volumes about the reputation and legacy of these two European explorers. To compare oneself to Balboa may communicate something quite different from the self-comparison to Cortez.[4]

Beyond the question of this trope's referentiality, however, is a larger question that I want my students to consider. What does it mean when we use other places, cultures, and histories primarily as a self-reflective mirror to give expression to our own states of mind? Is this the kind of imaginative travel that actually opens us up to the world of the other? As much as Keats's image of reading undoubtedly speaks to our own experiences (how many students majoring in English have been formed by hours of imaginative journeys to other lands?), this is a problematic way to love our neighbor. Does the privileging of the self and of self-discovery in this poem suggest the speaker to be animated less, to use Jacobs' terms, by the spirit of *caritas* toward others rather than by the *cupiditas* of self-awareness?

Anita Desai's short story "Scholar and Gypsy" raises similar questions about the ways in which we experience other cultures. This story features a married couple, David and Pat, who are in India while David completes his sociology thesis, and the story chronicles the slow implosion of their relationship, their longstanding problems exposed and exacerbated by the Indian setting. When teaching this story, I like to feature the formal structure of the story as a way of leading up to a thematic discussion of how these characters experience India. The story is almost perfectly balanced, as the action takes place in two settings: the cosmopolitan world of modern Bombay and the rural hill country of the north. As a class, we notice the series of contrasts defined by this geographical opposition between the sweltering heat of Bombay and the cool breezes of the northern hill country, and we talk about how these contrasts reveal character. David is most at home in Bombay, where he interacts with university peers and is socially affirmed, while Pat finds the heat and customs to be oppressive. The roles are reversed when they head north. Pat unexpectedly comes to life in an expatriate hippie subculture that lives in these foothills, while David finds himself out of sorts and reacts with petulant condescension.

The editors' prefatory comment, that through the chiasmic turn to the story "the scholar loses his way as the gypsy finds hers" (Desai, 2000, p. 2768), instigates a productive conversation about these two characters. I ask my students which of the two (if any) they identify with. Many of them sympathize with Pat and see in her story a familiar feminist narrative of the awakening of a woman whose identity has been repressed under her husband's paternalism. Certainly this reading finds ample support within the text. Few students identify with David, probably because the story ends with his most boorish behavior fresh in our memories. Several students will criticize both characters as ethnocentric (Pat's complaints about the "wild jungle stuff" she experiences in modern Bombay offer more than a hint of Orientalist condescension), turning our conversation toward the question of how these characters experience "India." Most students will find Pat's gypsy-like *joie de vivre* more appealing than David's pedantic self-importance. When David lectures Pat that what she took to be a Buddhist temple was in fact Hindu, these students will sympathize with her rejoinder that it is possible to find the spirit of Buddhism within a Hindu temple.

Still, it is fair to question whether either Pat or David has found anything more in India than what is familiar to them. Both characters may well deserve the epithet of "literary ecotourists" derogatively assigned by Susan Lanser to those "who dwell mentally in one or two (usually Western) countries, summer metaphorically in a third, and visit other places for brief interludes" (cited in Damrosch, 2003, p. 5). Perhaps neither David nor Pat has come into an authentic encounter with India as much as they have with the essentialized identity that they project onto India. It is not coincidental that the India with which each person identifies resembles the North American worlds in which they are individually at home – the cosmopolitan modernity of the Western academy for David and the rustic landscapes of New England for Pat.

Through the self-referential nature of these journeys to other lands, these works expose the problematic use of other settings primarily as a backdrop against which to define one's own experience. To love our neighbor, we must at least acknowledge our neighbor's presence.

Beyond Non-Judgmentalism

Every generation has its shibboleths, and non-judgmentalism seems to be one of ours. It is almost axiomatic in secondary and post-secondary education that it is bad form to judge another culture. Such judgment seems to be particularly out of bounds in the context of western Europe's sorry history of imperial conquest. In response to Chinua Achebe's brilliant postcolonial novel, *Things Fall Apart*, many of my students find it easy enough to give expression to lament, indignation, and elegiac appreciation for what the English colonizer destroyed. What does not come as easily – and often makes students uncomfortable – is to extend the ethical critique to elements of traditional Igbo culture, even those discomfiting characteristics that the novel portrays without sentimentality. To be sure, some students are appalled by the Igbo practice of leaving infant twins to die in the forest and can be dismissive of the culture as a whole, but other students seem hesitant even to express their personal disapproval of such practices. Perhaps these students wonder if they, as (for the most part) children of white and Western privilege, have any moral standing on which to critique a culture that has itself been victimized. While such ethical humility is understandable, we should be careful about limiting *a priori* who can and who cannot engage in ethical critique.

At any rate, these ethical discussions must be deferred until we have first paid attention to the world that, as the title indicates, is falling apart. I ask my students to read Part One in a way that some critics caution against – i.e., to approach the story as amateur anthropologists seeking to understand traditional Igbo ways of life. While Simon Gikandi (1991) writes of the "need to deconstruct the dominant view of the African novel as a source of ethnographic data" and reminds us that "novels, like all sources of knowledge, proffer incomplete and often contradictory perspectives" (p. 26), Emmanuel Obiechina (1991) points out that Achebe did intend "to restore the truth of a way of life that has been misrepresented over the centuries" (p. 31). As long as we recognize that the novel's portrayal of Igbo life is but a partial and a subjective portrait, I see such ethnographic observation as one of the ways in which we respectfully seek to understand the world of the Igbo.

We spend some class time documenting the rhythms of Igbo life: we observe structures of family life and the various roles assigned to parents and children; we discuss the social, political, and religious institutions of the society and the ways in which the tribe governs itself; we note the agricultural texture of life and the ways in which the calendar, religious practices, and daily habits revolve around the crops; we discuss the character traits and other values that are honored in this society. This sketch of traditional Igbo life serves several purposes. Perhaps most obviously, Achebe is pointedly reminding the West that a viable culture long predated the arrival of the European in these regions (cited in Gallagher, 2005, p. 336). Helping our students recognize the cultural institutions in a world they might otherwise dismiss as "primitive" teaches them of the variable forms that cultures can take. In terms of the plot, this amateur anthropology also prepares us for the dramatic changes that take place in Part Two, with the arrival of the white colonists. Only by recognizing the world that existed can we see how much is lost with the advent of colonial modernity. Finally, this attention to social norms and conventions prepares for a nuanced conversation about how Okonkwo is and is not representative of his society, a conversation that opens up to us Achebe's complex analysis of Igbo life, European colonialism, modernity, and Christianity.

The moral power of the novel naturally inspires lament and anger at the tragedies that unfold, and it is important to give students the chance to proclaim their indignation. Sometimes I'll ask them which character earns the dubious honor of the novel's greatest villain, a competitive category of nominees that usually includes the unnamed functionaries of the colonial judiciary, the district commissioner, and the overzealous missionary, Mr. Smith. These expressions of anger represent an important development in the moral ethos of the class. To love our neighbor includes the righteous anger that burns against oppression. But indignation does not represent the last word on the novel. Achebe has not written a sentimentalized treatise that reduces all Europeans to colonial predators and beatifies the Igbo as noble victims of injustice. To the contrary, the story is remarkably even-handed in recognizing the moral complexity of both Igbo society and the colonial presence.

Our discussion of Okonkwo helps us enter this morally complicated terrain. Achebe has created a flawed protagonist,[5] a man who suffers injustices perpetrated by those who will not recognize his humanity, but also a man whose excesses reveal that traditional life was not an unmitigated blessing for everyone. I first elicit personal responses to Okonkwo, with mixed results. Many admire his work ethic and accomplishments; some are offended by his severity toward his wives and children; nearly all are horrified that he takes Ikemefuna's fate into his own hands; and nearly all feel sorry for him when he is banished for the accident that kills his kinsman. In these discussions, students often wonder if their own judgments are culturally appropriate (especially in relation to his behavior as husband and father), so I ask them what kinds of judgments about Okonkwo are formed by respected elders like Obierika. At such moments, the class can enact a hermeneutical dialogue similar to the "elliptical refractions" to which Damrosch refers, as we compare our reactions to the judgments formed by cultural insiders like Obierika. These are the conversations in which the assertion of cultural difference does not stop conversation but rather draws us into genuine dialogue with what turn out to be multiple perspectives even in the novel. It becomes possible to see that Okonkwo does not speak for all of the Igbo, both in his construction of masculinity and in his response to societal change.

This narrative complexity is also apparent in the novel's depiction of traditional Igbo customs. While the agrarian rhythms of hard work and communal feasts celebrate the dignity and beauty of an ancient culture, Achebe does not gloss over the harsher realities of life in this world. Our discussion of the treatment of twins and outcasts, as well as the judicial practices that create scapegoats like Ikemefuna, usually becomes quite spirited. Typically, infanticide reveals the limits of tolerance to which most students will go in the name of cultural diversity, but occasionally someone will defend the relativist injunction that we have no business criticizing the moral practices of another culture. Such students should be respected for their courage, but I also want to challenge them to consider whether there are any cultural practices that would justify external humanitarian interventions. Does the command to love one's neighbor ever justify an infringement upon certain cultural practices?

When we do not exempt certain cultures from moral scrutiny but treat all cultures (including our own) with a moral seriousness, the resulting conversation gains in depth and richness. Treating one's neighbor (whether collectively as a culture or as individual humans) as responsible agents whom we respect enough to question is an indispensable part of loving our neighbor as ourselves. Within a Christian ethic, we cannot divide cultures or human beings into predetermined categories of the virtuous and the fallen. *Things Fall Apart* reminds us that cultures, like humans, represent a complex mixture of good and evil. Just as neither Igbo nor European cultures should be dismissed as irredeemable, so too should neither culture be spared moral critique where appropriate.

A Reconciling Love

This essay has been drawing out the implications of a hermeneutic of love for our reading of world literature, and we conclude now by considering a novel that brings a disparate group of Japanese travelers on a pilgrimage to India, ostensibly to view sacred Buddhist sites but really, *pace* Foster, on various quests to find love and emotional healing. This novel, too, foregrounds religious and cultural diversity but multiplies binarisms into a three-dimensional kaleidoscope of difference: we discover Japanese honeymooners and a seminarian in France; Japanese tourists in India; various deities and symbols from Buddhism, Hinduism, and Christianity; and the political and religious tensions that led to the assassination of Indira Gandhi (which figures in the story). At the center of the story is one of the most iconoclastic figures in all of literature: an expatriate Japanese priest, alienated from his native land and the "Eurocentric" Catholic Church he serves, living in a Hindu ashram and dressing like a Brahman so that he might bring the dying untouchables to the sacred river Ganges. Both the assassination of Gandhi and the riot that erupts over a Japanese tourist's cultural insensitivity give these expressions of diversity a darker edge. They seem less a cause for celebration than a symptom of humanity's propensity toward sectarian violence. But it is out of this messy cauldron of human differences that novelist Shusaku Endo offers poignant glimpses of a love that heals and reconciles. This love becomes figured both through the odd character of Otsu and through the syncretistic symbol of the River Ganges, which quietly absorbs the endless flow of humanity in its embracing waters.

As with *Things Fall Apart*, the characters in this novel invite immediate comment. For characters who are as culturally and personally idiosyncratic as are Endo's creations, it is remarkable how easily my students come to identify with them. Numada, the writer of children's books inhabited by talking animals, believes that a myna bird once died in his place. The war veteran Kiguchi lives with harrowing memories of the brutal Burma death march. Isobe is a recently widowed Japanese salaryman who comes to India on a quixotic quest to seek his late wife's reincarnated self. Mitsuko Naruse enacts the pathologies of fictional characters, seducing Otsu out of spite and finding an odd alter-ego in a François Mauriac character who murders her respectable husband. Despite all of these markers of difference from my students' typical experiences, they are deeply moved by the loneliness and alienation experienced by these characters. My students' responses to these characters echo the comment made by Achebe that he encounters readers of varied races who tell him that Okonkwo is just like their fathers (Achebe, 1991, pp. 21-22). These discussions of character give us a chance to listen to and understand the particular anguish of each character and to see how the narrative resolves their hearts' longings.

It is the religious subtext of the novel that I am most drawn to and that helps us probe the complex intersections of religion and culture. I usually provide some biographical background on Endo to help students recognize that Otsu's frustrations with what he calls European Christianity echo some of Endo's perennial concerns.[6] Endo's oft-repeated metaphor, that when he was baptized at the age of ten he was given a Western-style suit that did not fit his Japanese body (see

Mathy, 1992, p. 66), resonates with students, who themselves are often trying to distill the spirit of Christianity from its cultural residue. We turn to Otsu's critique of Christianity (Endo, 1994, pp. 117-122) and talk about whether he is right that Christianity is overly rational and systematic. If so, does that rationality alienate someone like Otsu, who describes himself as an "Asian [who] just can't make sharp distinctions and pass judgment on everything the way [the European priests] do" (Endo, 1994, p. 118)? Often students initially respond sympathetically to Otsu, but these comments themselves have a certain anti-institutional bias that locates the theological problem primarily with scholastic Catholic theology. When I press them about what theological affirmations they would be willing to jettison and which ones are non-negotiable, the conversation becomes much more complex, and they wonder to what extent Otsu (and Endo) are merely seeking a corrective from an overly-rational theological system or are pressing much more radically toward a pluralistic, non-theological spirituality. When I mention that Endo had been influenced by John Hick's notion of religious pluralism during the composition of *Deep River* (cited in Hick, 2000, p. 286), and when we consider Otsu's leanings toward a religious universalism (Endo, 1994, pp. 121-122, 184), the conversation moves to a new level of complexity as we consider the difficult question of whether the Christian gospel is truly universal or merely culturally contingent. It is at this point in the course that many students come to recognize most fully that certain kinds of argument for cultural diversity presume that religion is itself but a subset of culture and therefore culturally relative. This is not the point at which I hope my students remain, but I do think it is important for them to wrestle with the question of whether all assertions of cultural diversity are consistent with confessional affirmations of Christ as Redeemer of the entire cosmos.

Lest it seem that the course discussion at this point has digressed into purely theological concerns, let me return to the novel's thematic and character concerns. The novel works its way imagistically and thematically toward the notion of reconciliation, symbolized by the great river that attracts these characters and invites them into its healing waters. Most of the characters take at least some small steps outside the bounds of their egotism and begin to exercise the capacity to love others. We talk about what has helped these characters learn to love, and we look at passages in which Otsu compares the love of his "Onion"[7] to the love of a mother (Endo, 1994, p. 119) and in which the tour guide impassionedly speaks of the long-suffering love of the goddess Chamunda (pp. 139-140). We talk about Mitsuko's recognition that she has settled for counterfeits of love and that she now longs for the genuine article (p. 161). Above all, we talk about the radical, self-denying love of Otsu that impels him to perform the most humble and, from a pragmatic point of view, apparently pointless acts of love in carrying the dying to the funeral pyres along the banks of the Ganges. These discussions about love help us to recognize that, in spite of different cultural conventions about how love might be expressed, the need to love and to be loved seems to transcend cultural boundaries.

What authorizes such love in this novel? Some of my students are frustrated by the novel's indeterminate refusal to answer that question definitively. That indeterminacy is symbolized most clearly by the exchange between Mitsuko and a Sister of Mercy who is ministering to a dying woman in the streets. When Mitsuko asks the nun why she does this work, the nun replies, "Because except for this ... there is nothing in this world we can believe in" (p. 215). Actually, Mitsuko does not hear if the pronoun is "this" or "him," a distinction that could mean that this love is authorized as a general humanitarian impulse or through the self-giving love of the "Onion." Does the novel sustain the argument that all roads lead to God, or is there a primacy to the love of the Onion? What do we make of the repeated refrains from Isaiah 53, and does it matter that those refrains always end in the middle of verse four, omitting subsequent references to the suffering servant's being "wounded for our transgressions" and "bruised for our iniquities" (Isa 53:5 RSV)? What do the repeated symbolic allusions to sacraments like confession, the Eucharist, and baptism suggest in the novel?

While the novel may not provide as much closure to the preceding religious questions as many readers might wish, *Deep River* nevertheless leaves us with a powerful image in Otsu of a love so radically oriented to enacting the love of the "Onion" that he will serve the most despised members of the human race. This is not a bad image with which to end a course that challenges us to love our neighbor.

By the time we have finished this course, I want my students to have thought more deeply about the ways in which they think about cultural difference. Have they been able to enter into the refracted spaces in which it is possible to dialogue through our respective cultural particularities? Have our imaginative journeys to exotic lands and cultures served merely to satisfy our own curiosity, or have they brought us into a genuine encounter with others? Can they bring a respectful and ethically-attentive judgment to their engagement with culture? Most of all, though this is an objective that defies easy assessment, have they grown in their capacity to love others and to seek their well-being?

Notes

1   Damrosch uses the term *national* quite broadly to account for a variety of local and ethnic groups that long preceded the origins of the modern nation state (p. 283).

2   Charles J. Rzepka has recently surveyed the full debate and argues that the substitution was intentional. Thomas Frosch makes a different case that the reference to Cortez was not an error but a "Freudian parapraxis" that represents Keats's repressed "predatory ambition to obliterate Homer and to be in his place," a desire better signified by the analogy to Cortez than to Balboa (Frosch, 2004, p. 149). While I am not persuaded of the intentionality of this substitution, my argument is less about whether Keats meant "Cortez" than by the way in which that allusion functions in this text more as a self-referential marker for the speaker than as a reference to the lived human experience of the lands to which the poet travels vicariously through literature.

3   The footnote reads as follows: "There is no reason to agree with Tennyson that Cortez is a mistake for Balboa (the first European to see the Pacific Ocean), and a sign of Keats's inferior education" (Damrosch, 2006, p. 924).

4   The history of the European conquest of what is present-day Latin America is by any account a story of considerable brutality and bloodshed. While Vasco Núñez de

Balboa's establishment of the first European settlement in Central America was not without its own cruelties, Hernán Cortés is remembered as a particularly ruthless conquistador for his defeat of the Aztec empire and the emperor Moctezuma. And while the reasons for their divergent reputations are far too complex to investigate in these pages, Balboa is seen and celebrated as the founder of what would become Panama whereas Cortés has come to be identified, particularly in the twentieth-century, as the destroyer of the indigenous Aztec culture. One symbolic measure of the divergent reputations of these two conquistadors is the artwork that commemorates these two men. In Panama City, a large statue of Balboa prominently graces the Avenida Balboa. No such statue of Cortés exists in Mexico, but Cortés is unflatteringly depicted in several prominent murals by the great painters Diego Rivera and José Clemente Orozco. Rivera's epic mural *The History of Mexico*, which adorns the walls of the National Palace, creates a morally unambiguous history of Mexico, which associates the good with the indigenous Aztec culture and the evil with Cortés's "invasion, subjugation, and exploitation" (Rochfort, 2006, p. 51). Rochfort describes Orozco's paintings (*Dimensions* and *The Violence of Conquest*) as a symbol of "white European Renaissance man at his most aggressive, acquisitive, and violent" (Rochfort, 2006, p. 51). A further symbol of Cortés' opprobrium in present-day Mexico is the expression "la malinchista," which is derived from the name of Cortés' translator and consort, Doña Marina (aka La Malinche), and which is a synonym for traitor or a "lover of foreigners" (Krauss, 1997, p. 4).

5   In "Teaching *Things Fall Apart*," Achebe acknowledges that many readers are disturbed that Okonkwo fails: "I have been asked this question in one form or another by a certain kind of reader for thirty years: Why did you allow a just cause to stumble and fall? The best I can do for an answer is to say that it is in the nature of things .... Good causes can and do fail even when the people who espouse and lead them are not themselves in one way or another severely flawed. This theme is of course the stuff of tragedy in literature and is well-known" (pp. 22-23).

6   For a brief introduction to Endo's history, readers may wish to consult Francis Mathy's "Shusaku Endo: Japanese Catholic Novelist," in *America*. Van C. Gessel and Mark Williams have reminded Endo's Western readers of the historical and literary milieu out of which Endo emerged. In "Voices in the Wilderness," "Endo Shusaku: His Position(s) in Postwar Japanese Literature," and *The Sting of Life*, Gessel situates Endo in the "Third Generation" writers who came of age during the Second World War. Williams's *Endo Shusaku: A Literature of Reconciliation* provides one of the most extensive explanations of the complex interrelationship of the author's life and fiction (pp. 25-57).

7   Because of Mitsuko's impatience with conventional theological language, Otsu proposes the arbitrary term "the Onion" as an alternative to the word "God."

Bibliography

Abrams, M. H., et al. (Eds.). (1993). *The Norton anthology of English literature* (6th ed., Vol. 2). New York: Norton.

Abrams, M. H., et al. (Eds.). (2000). *The Norton anthology of English literature* (7th ed., Vol. 2). New York and London: Norton.

Achebe, C. (1991). Teaching *Things fall apart*. In Bernth Lindfors (Ed.), *Approaches to teaching Achebe's* Things fall apart (pp. 20-24). New York: MLA.

Achebe, C. (1994) *Things fall apart*. New York: Anchor Books.

Appiah, K. A. (2006). *Cosmopolitanism: Ethics in a world of strangers*. New York and London: Norton.

Calvin College. (2004). *From every nation: Revised comprehensive plan for racial justice, reconciliation, and cross-cultural engagement at Calvin College.* Grand Rapids, MI: Calvin College. Retrieved May 30, 2007, from the Calvin College Web site: http://www.calvin.edu/admin/provost/multicultural/documents/FEN.pdf.

Damrosch, D. (2003). *What is world literature?* Princeton: Princeton University.

Damrosch, D., et al. (2006). *The Longman anthology of British literature* (3rd ed., Vol. 2A). New York: Pearson Longman.

Desai, A. (2000). Scholar and gypsy. In M. L. Abrams, et al. (Eds.), *The Norton anthology of English literature* (7th ed., Vol. 2, pp. 2768-2785). New York and London: Norton.

Endo, S. (1994). *Deep river* (Van C. Gessel, Trans.). New York: New Directions.

Foster, T. (2003). *How to read literature like a professor: A lively and entertaining guide to reading between the lines.* New York: Quill.

Frosch, T. (2004). In Keats's On first looking into Chapman's Homer. *The Explicator, 62*(3), 146-150.

Gadamer, H. G. (1989). *Truth and method* (2nd ed., J. Weinsheimer & D. G. Marshall, Trans.). New York: Crossroad.

Gallagher, S. (2005, Spring). Reading and faith in a global community. *Christianity & Literature, 54,* 323-340.

Gessel, V. C. (1982, Winter). Voices in the wilderness: Japanese Christian authors. *Monumenta Nipponica, 37*(4), 437-457.

Gessel, V. C. (1989). *The sting of life: Four contemporary Japanese novelists.* New York: Columbia University.

Gikandi, S. (1991). Chinua Achebe and the signs of the times. In Bernth Lindfors (Ed.), *Approaches to teaching Achebe's* Things fall apart (pp. 25-30). New York: MLA.

Hick, J. (2002). *John Hick: An autobiography.* Oxford: One World.

Jacobs, A. (2001). *A theology of reading: The hermeneutics of love.* Cambridge, MA: Westview.

Keats, J. (2006). On first reading Chapman's Homer. In J. Stillinger & D. S. Lynch (Eds.), *The Norton anthology of English literature* (8th ed., Vol. D, pp. 880-881). New York and London: Norton.

Krauss, Clifford. (1997, March 25). After 500 years, Cortes's girlfriend is not forgiven. *The New York Times* (Section A, Page 4, Column 3). Retrieved June 13, 2007, from LexisNexis ™ Academic: http://web.lexis-nexis.com/universe/document?_m=2b87e93e4b2c8983d929d0f20c387a82&_docnum=1&wchp=dGLzVlz-zSkVA&_md5=249a33fe231341fa09a9f7dfe652a6d5

Mathy, F., S. J. (1992, August 8). Shusaku Endo: Japanese Catholic novelist. *America,* 66-71.

Obiechina, E. (1991). Following the author in *Things fall apart.* In Bernth Lindfors (Ed.), *Approaches to teaching Achebe's* Things fall apart (pp. 31-37). New York: MLA.

Rochfort, Desmond. (2006). The sickle, the serpent, and the soil. In Mary Kay Vaughan and Stephen E. Lewis (Eds.), *The eagle and the virgin* (pp. 43-57). Durham and London: Duke University.

Rzepka, C. J. (2002) "Cortez – or Balboa, or somebody like that": Form, fact, and forgetting in Keats's "Chapman's Homer" sonnet. *Keats-Shelley Journal,* 51, 35-75.

Said, E. (1978). *Orientalism.* New York: Vintage.

Said, E. (1994). The politics of knowledge. In R. C. Davis & R. Schleifer (Eds.), *Contemporary literary criticism: Literary and cultural studies* (3rd ed., pp. 145-153). New York: Longman.

Smith, D. I., & Carvill, B. (2000). *The gift of the stranger: Faith, hospitality, and foreign language learning.* Grand Rapids, MI: Eerdmans.

Stillinger, J., & Lynch, D. S. (Eds.). (2006). *The Norton anthology of English literature* (8th ed., Vol. D). New York and London: Norton.

Williams, M. (1999). *Endo Shusaku: A literature of reconciliation*. London and New York: Routledge.

JE&CB 11:2 (2007) 83-94   1366-5456

Mark A. Pike

Transactional Reading as Spiritual Investment

THIS ARTICLE ADDRESSES how Christians can read wisely and well as citizens of both God's kingdom and an increasingly secular society. I suggest that focussing on reading as a transaction between reader and text rather than on the morality of texts or the maturity of readers can provide a biblical approach for Christian educators seeking to invest reading experiences with Christian faith. I also contend that reading is one of the ways Christians should invest in a secular society and that when readers sow their faith and invest their spiritual lives in their reading transactions, they can grow spiritually.

This article seeks biblical answers to some of the questions Christian parents and teachers ask (or should be asking) about their children's reading: What should be read? What should not be read? How should a child's reading be guided? How can the spiritual direction in which a text inclines a reader be discerned? How can young readers apply their faith to their reading? How can teachers and parents foster readers who are spiritually keen, perceptive and well-motivated? How can young readers be helped to read rightly as disciples of Jesus Christ? Here I consider how parents and teachers can help children read wisely and well as citizens both of God's kingdom and of an increasingly secular society.

By focussing here on reading as a transaction, I seek to move us beyond the polarities of freedom and restraint, parents' direction and children's obedience, teacher's authority and pupil's submission, autonomy and heteronomy, public and private, aesthetic and efferent, reason and feelings, and so on. Transactions between readers and texts are more significant spiritually than most Christians realise because readers do not learn to read and *then* form a worldview; they do so *while* they are reading. Before going any further, perhaps I should begin to indicate what I have in mind when I refer to reading as a transaction and a spiritual investment. I shall take each in turn.

Rosenblatt's transactional theory of the literary work[1] will be drawn upon here and is valuable because it demonstrates that the educator's focus cannot rightly be on *either* the text *or* the reader but has to be on what happens when *both* come together. This is significant because it means the teaching of reading cannot rightly be based on the features of a text *or* the character of a reader but on the nature of transactions *between* text and reader. As 'reading is transactional, the type of reading that occurs is ... co-determined by the nature of the text and the stance of the reader' (Smith, 2004, p. 144). Transactional theory is redolent of the Gospel of Matthew's parable of the sower,[2] in which we learn about good soil and good seed being required for spiritual growth. Sowing and reaping is a biblical metaphor, and Christians should seek to discern what happens when a work of fiction is planted in the imagination of a reader and words carrying meaning are sown in the spirit of a child.

Attention to reading as a transaction can provide a biblical approach for those seeking to invest reading experiences with their Christian faith. By 'spiritual investment' I am indicating that Christian readers need to render their reading to God; they need to invest their Christian faith, beliefs and commitments in the reading transaction rather than reading literature as if they were secular readers and not Christians at all. We recall that when Jesus was asked, 'Is it lawful to give tribute unto Caesar, or not?' he responded by asking whose image and inscription was on the tribute money; when he was told it was Caesar's, he replied to those who were trying to trick him, 'Render therefore unto Caesar the things which are Caesar's; and unto God the things that are God's' (Matt 22:21b KJV). I contend here that faithful reading (reading in which faith is invested) is owed to God. The ability to read is one of the most remarkable gifts God has given to his people, enduing us with the ability not only to decode and translate graphemes into phonemes but also to interpret and respond. I have referred to this previously as the spiritual gift of reading (Pike, 2004d); we are made in God's image and it is our reasonable service, as Christians, to read with integrity and to acknowledge Him whenever we read. We should render our reading to God, but reading is to be a spiritual investment rather than just the payment of a debt we owe.

Reading is not only a gift we have received but also something we can sow (the notion of transaction is once again apt). There has to be an investment of one's talents, a giving of oneself, if faith is to be applied to reading.[3] To read with integrity as Christians means investing our faith and spiritual life in the texts we encounter. Far more than an awareness of the features of different genres is required. In readers' responses to character, theme and language can be found their verdicts upon the world and views of what is worthwhile. Yet in our society even the activity of teaching reading has become secularised with an emphasis on improving skills rather than understanding the beliefs and values promoted by texts (Pike, 2006).[4] This is a very different conception of literacy from that privileged by earlier generations of Christian educators who understood the importance of biblical teaching and Christian values being integrated from a child's first encounter with the letters ABC.[5] Christian readers need to be encouraged to apply their faith to their reading[6] but also need help to discern what their responses to their reading reveal about their faith, values and commitments.

The schools that many Christian children attend often encourage (or even require) them to read texts promoting values that conflict with those of their Christian homes.[7] Reading is not neutral, and when young people engage with such texts, their beliefs about what is morally acceptable can be influenced and the direction of their lives altered. If Christian parents and teachers are reticent about influencing their children's reading, they should be aware that many non-Christians in government, education, the media and commercial publishing have no such qualms. Too many Christian parents and teachers seem to be influenced more by the emphasis in contemporary culture on children's rights than by biblical teaching emphasizing their obligation to provide pervasive Christian nurture. Exercising discernment regarding the reading of young readers is an important responsibility, yet many Christian parents and teachers seem to lack the confidence or commitment to invest time in their children's reading transactions. Some make the mistake of focussing on a child's personal devotional life rather than seeing the relevance of faith to reading, and many Christian teachers have grown so accustomed to segregating their Christian commitments from the texts they teach that they are unperturbed by the insidious secularisation of education and consider it normal. Even Christian schools can be insufficiently discriminating regarding reading, preferring to emphasize ethos or make statements about promoting a Christian worldview rather than engaging with the detail of what it might be to read a range of texts in the classroom from a Christian perspective (rather than a Marxist or feminist one for instance).

Readers

Jesus told his disciples that when they lived and remained in him and his words lived and remained in them, they would *ask* rightly.[8] W. H. Auden suggests that instead of asking 'What can I know?' we should ask 'What, at this moment, am I meant to know?' (Auden, 1962, p. 272) and Christian parents and teachers can help young disciples ask 'What would God have me read?' or 'What is it good for me to read?' When Jesus' present-day disciples live and remain in him and his words live and remain in them, they will *read* rightly and ask the right questions concerning their reading.[9] In practice, readers cannot read rightly if they segregate their reading from their believing. Christian readers are called to engage in all reading transactions in the light of their transactions with Scripture and their relationship with Jesus Christ.

Understanding the nature of the transaction between text and reader is especially important as we live in a society where an assortment of texts seek to instruct impressionable young people how they should behave and the attitudes they should adopt. Recent literacy research concludes that 'where earlier generations of children were socialized primarily within the boundaries of family, school, religious organization and community, consumer and popular culture is now the principal mode of early childhood socialization' (Luke, Carrington, & Kapitzke, 2003, p. 254). For many readers in a secular society, such texts have replaced written biblical revelation to interpret life, and Christians often exert little or no control over the texts and images of mainstream culture that they and their children are bombarded with on a daily basis. It seems that in 'our culture, we have accepted that the right to know is absolute and unlimited'; as a consequence, the freedom not to know (or not to want to know) is less frequently exercised by Christians than is spiritually healthy: 'We are quite prepared to admit that, while sex and food are good in themselves, an uncontrolled pursuit of either is not, but it is difficult for us to believe that intellectual curiosity is a desire like any other' (Auden, 1962, p. 272). Moral reading is not well served by the unlimited access to the range of texts that our information age provides through sources such as the Internet.

In this context it is important that children learn to accept guidance. It is not always in the child's best interests to exercise autonomy, nor is it consistent with

Christian nurture to allow complete freedom concerning text choice. Yet Christian educators know they have to prepare children to make their own wise reading choices. This begs two important questions: When are Christian parents and teachers to allow choice and freedom, and when should they impose restraint or direction? On what basis should these decisions to be made? It has recently been argued that we should aim at 'producing *rational*, well-balanced people willing and able to exercise independent judgement, rely on expert advice or submit to legitimate authority as the occasion demands' (Hand, 2006, p. 539; italics mine). Making decisions about whether to submit to authority or act independently on the basis of *reason* alone will, however, be considered inadequate by Christians seeking to act on the basis of their God-given reason but also in response to their own transactional reading of biblical texts concerning the spiritual development of their children:

> The concept of having to be a certain sort of person, morally or theologically, in order to read a book aright – with the implication that perhaps, if one is not that sort of person, then the book should be withheld from one – is alien to the assumption of liberal modernity that every rational adult should be free and is able to read every book. (MacIntyre, 1990, p. 133)

Such a perspective is more congruent with a biblical application of transactional reading theory than the one-sided assertion that the 'reader is the final arbiter of a text's morality' (Gallagher & Lundin, 1989, p. 140) or the claim that 'it is the reader's will that determines the moral form the reading takes' (Jacobs, 2001, p. 31). With regard to children and adolescents, to suggest that the reader 'determines' the morality of the text seems foolhardy. Some adults, like Augustine, may be able and willing 'to reconfigure a reading experience in order to profit, spiritually and morally, from it' (Jacobs, 2001, p. 23), but it is important to take into account the ways in which young readers who have 'not yet arrived at a consistent view of life' (Rosenblatt, 1968, p. 31) respond to certain texts at particular points in their lives.

Readers (and those responsible for guiding them) do not always know how they will respond to particular texts or how they will be inclined to believe or behave during and after reading. Readers are not always aware during the reading event what they will retain after it. According to Rosenblatt it is efferent reading (from the Latin *effere*, to carry away) that occurs when the reader reads in order to extract information to be retained after reading but I would contend that it is when readers think their primary purpose is fulfilled *during* the reading event (which Rosenblatt refers to as aesthetic reading) that they may carry away more than they bargained for. We do not always know what goes on spiritually when readers are immersed in texts or even when they believe only information is being extracted. As 'we do not approach every encounter with the printed word anticipating that it will result in new insights into the nature of belief', there is the possibility the literature will 'catch the reader off guard' (Nichols, 2000, p. 3) especially when 'almost no one seems to have considered reading of non-biblical texts a theologically significant activity' (Jacobs, 2001, p. 111).

Whether readers are aware of it or not, however, reading is a theologically significant activity, and C. S. Lewis addresses this issue in *The Abolition of Man*, alternatively entitled *Reflections on education with special reference to the teaching of English in the upper forms of schools.* (Lewis, 1943/1978).[10] Lewis reviews a school text he calls 'The Green Book' (to preserve its authors' anonymity) and cogently argues that while the reader is not overtly or explicitly taught a theory about life, certain worldview-assumptions implicit in the text are likely to exert an unseen but profound influence. The values implicit in the text are so potent because they are latent. The influence of the book is subtle and yet Lewis discerns clear 'Disapprovals' and 'Approvals' in the worldview of the authors, who reflect 'the whole system of values which happened to be in vogue' in their circles at the time of writing (p. 61). He argues that an assumption planted in a person when reading a text while at school can condition behaviour ten years later and cause the individual to adopt one position rather than another even though the origin of the assumption is unconscious and long forgotten. The outcomes of readers' transactions with texts can be far reaching.

Texts

It has been suggested that a 'good book has a profound kind of morality ... which inspires the reader's inner life and draws out all that is noble' (Hunt, 1989, p. 40), which is clearly redolent of Paul's injunction to think on things that are true, honest, just, pure, lovely and virtuous (Phil 4:8). Christian educators certainly need to encourage children and young people to read works by Christian writers of good quality literature that affirm 'the goodness of imagination, make-believe, intrigue, humour, flair and mystery but within the framework of a life-affirming biblical worldview' (Roques, 1989, p. 98). But they need to do more than this. When a 'powerful and prophetic Christian perspective is almost never presented' (Roques, 1989, p. 94) in most popular children's literature and the texts read by young readers do not offer a depiction of the world from a Christian viewpoint,[11] it is important to help readers discern underlying values in their reading – especially when non-Christian ways of living and thinking are implicit and assumed by authors to be shared by their readers.[12]

Christians can all too easily object only to obviously coarse language or blatant sexual immorality in texts, when works without such noticeable features can influence young readers for ill. Teachers and parents need to think about whether the values promoted by particular characters, plots, authors and descriptions run counter to the values they wish to promote in their schools and homes. Arguably,

> The type of book which perhaps requires most care in censoring is not that which is obviously of poor quality, or containing bad language, or written by an author with a dubious occult or sexual agenda, but by one whose mindset and general perspective on the world is not Christian. Values are always communicated in literature – it cannot be neutral. (McClean, 1999, p. 11)

While parents should not be afraid to censor certain texts, they should bear in mind that censoring a book that promotes non-Christian values and is founded upon a non-Christian worldview might not always be the best way of enabling young readers to engage with their non-Christian culture.

For Christian readers to read only books where the values promoted are the same as their own may not provide the best preparation for life or an understanding of those with different beliefs.[13] Reading works either by authors who do not have a Christian worldview or about the lives of those with whom Christian readers profoundly disagree can be valuable but is safest in a supportive Christian context, for being 'in the world but not of it means knowing about and investigating the values and ideas of secularism, without being driven and shaped by them' (Ireland, 2004, p. 58). Parents and teachers need to gauge when their children are ready to investigate values and ways of living which are anti-Christian in order to engage with a fallen world, as there is the risk of readers being influenced and shaped by texts which present unrighteous living as alluring and appealing. For Christian parents and teachers, focussing on the transaction between reader and text is vital if children and teenagers are to be protected from, and prepared to live in, their world. The indeterminacy of literature allows 'the reader to place himself within the world of the fiction' (Iser, 1971, p. 44), and it is this capacity of literature to help readers access other worlds through vicarious experience that is so valuable. As Christians, we are called to enter other worlds. Specifically, we are called to reach out to this temporal world and invest our lives in it while not being conformed to it (Pike, 2005b).

I have previously suggested that the aesthetic distance (or difference) between the text and reader has the potential to map out the terrain across which spiritual journeys can be made (Pike, 2002b). We need to recognize, though, that some texts are more likely than others to set the reader up to travel towards God. It is important to consider 'the spiritual direction in which a work inclines' (Jacobs, 2001, p. 22); the parables Jesus told shocked, left questions unanswered and propelled his listeners into spiritual, mental and even physical activity, but they had the potential to set people off on spiritual journeys that led in the direction of the Father (Pike, 2003d). Many popular texts today incline young readers to travel in the opposite direction.

Transactions

Christians have a responsibility to teach their children how to adopt a Christian stance to their reading as well as life: 'We must do more than live in the same house with our children. We need to spend time with them, talk to them, share our lives with them, and teach them .... Influencing our children is not a casual task. It won't get done unless we have a plan' (Hunt, 1989, p. 110). A central element of any plan, for Christians, should be to respond to all reading transactions in the light of the most significant reading transaction of all. Christians are called to apply their transactions with Scripture to their transactions with all of the texts they encounter. Guided transactions (in the sense that they are guided by the Holy Spirit) can enable Christian educators to move beyond a focus on the morality of texts or the maturity of readers and to understand that a work of the imagination affects one's 'moral and religious existence' (Eliot, 1935, p. 396).

Bridget Nicols (2000) suggests something approaching transactional theory when she observes that readers participate in a two-way engagement with literature:

> Setting out to read in the light of faith is one part of it. Finding that we ourselves are being 'read' by the texts we study, so that our preconceptions and certainties are laid out for fresh examination, is the other part. 'Reading faithfully' means being open to both parts of the process. (pp. 4-5)

The task for Christian educators is far more complex than banning certain books; the reading curriculum needs to be designed not only according to features of texts but also according to the features of *transactions* with texts.[14] A Christian perspective on reading necessarily sees the spiritual and moral aspects of the transaction and the importance of acknowledging rather than eschewing or secularising these. Rosenblatt's account, while asserting the importance of the reader's experience of life and sense of values, is secular.[15] It falls considerably short of acknowledging that if 'attention to God does not *precede* and *envelop* our observations of the world, then those observations are simply idolatrous' (Jacobs, 2001, p. 21).

Teachers and parents need to perceive how a reader is responding to a text, how a worldview is being formed, how faith is growing and whether behaviour is becoming more Christ-like. When 'someone ... knows what is best for him or her to do, but nonetheless does not act accordingly', this may be due to 'some imperfection in that person's knowledge' or 'some imperfection in the education and disciplining of the passions' (MacIntyre, 1988, p.156). Reading transactions can play a part in such disciplining passions but response to literature can also reveal the extent to which passions have been disciplined. For Augustine, 'the will is governed by what it loves: love determines will, and will in turn ... governs interpretation' (Jacobs, 2001, p. 45). When a society that loves its own secularism assumes that young Christian readers should divorce their reading from their faith, it takes courage to read as a Christian.

While reader response theorists[16] acknowledge that the background of the reader (for instance, gender, politics, ethnicity, socio-economic context or specific life experience) influences response and interpretation, they rarely legitimate religious or faith-based perspectives (explicitly at least). The secularism of this is only too obvious, and yet 'the author of a work of imagination is trying to affect us wholly, as human beings' (Eliot, 1935, p. 394). Bringing Christian conviction to the reading process renders intellectual honesty to Caesar, the secular society, and can provide the opportunity for its readers to exchange meanings, interpretations and responses with those whose lives are invested with a Christian worldview. A denial of faith in the reading transaction can lead to a painful spiritual bankruptcy; we are not called to adopt the stance of Peter, who denied any personal relationship with Jesus when it seemed politically expedient.

In this article I have argued that, for Christians, all reading transactions are to take place in the light of their personal transactions with Scripture. Yet 'the main legacy of modern liberalism' is that 'many if not most citizens of contemporary liberal democracies cannot take religious stories and narratives seriously' (Carr, 2004, p. 391). Such a reading environment encourages children to conform to the majority values of the secular state. It is vital, however, for a liberal society to take faith seriously and to encourage reading informed by the Christian faith in the public domain even if these interpretations are contested.[17] Christian readers are a minority 'within the dominant liberal life-world' (Wright, 2003, p. 148), and we should be aware that their responses can be limited by 'teachers with anti-religious views and school policies which assume a secularist view of religion or are insensitive to families from religious backgrounds' (Jackson, 2003, p. 96). If young Christian readers are not encouraged to connect their faith with their reading (as is the case in many secular classrooms), reading transactions will become secularized. This bodes ill for a society that needs to understand and tolerate perspectives other than its own.[18] Educators from a variety of persuasions need to accept the fact that Christians' reading belongs to God.

Acknowledgements

I should like to thank David Smith, Leslie Mosher, Michael Jennings, Stephanie Cribb, John Kershaw and Phill Moon for thought-provoking discussion on what it is to engage in reading and the teaching of reading as a Christian. I should also like to thank the anonymous reviewers of this journal for their detailed comments on an earlier draft of this paper.

Notes

1   Rosenblatt was Professor of English Education at New York University and is better known in the US than the UK. Key works are *Literature as Exploration* (London: Heinemann, 1968), first published in 1938 and republished in 1968, 1976, 1983, and 1995; "The Transactional Theory of the Literary Work: Implications for Research" in C. R. Cooper (ed.) *Researching Response to Literature and the Teaching of Literature: Points of Departure* (Norwood, NY: Ablex, 1985); *The Reader, the Text, the Poem: The Transactional Theory of the Literary Work: With a New Preface and Epilogue* (Carbondale, IL: Southern Illinois University Press, 1994); and *Making Meaning with Texts: Selected Essays* (Portsmouth, NH: Heinemann, 2005).

2   See Pike (2003) for a more detailed exploration of the relation between Rosenblatt's transactional theory and the Matthean parable of the sower. It is significant that Jesus indicates that understanding this parable is a key to understanding his other parables: 'And he said unto them, Know ye not this parable? And how then will ye know all parables? The sower soweth the word' (Mark 4:13-14).

3   Responding to text as 'stimulus' where "the reader brings to or adds to the non-verbal or socio-physical setting, *his whole past experience of life and literature*" (Rosenblatt, 1978, p. 8; my italics) requires a certain vulnerability, openness and honesty whereby one brings one's life to the text and allows the text to evoke memories, associations and so on. A good way to start is to encourage Christian readers to annotate a text with faith-based comments rather than aspects of style or language. This can be modelled for them and shows how a Christian worldview can be ap-

plied to a text. Such an approach legitimates their faith and stance as Christian rather than secular readers. However, it can take some time to adjust to and needs to be practiced regularly. See also Pike (2000a) and Pike (2000b).

4   There is a far greater emphasis in national UK literacy policy on improving skills than there is on discerning values in texts. See Hall (2003) and Hilton (2003). If discerning values in texts is important and the curriculum is a text children innocently read, we should help them see the values underpinning the subjects they study. In Halstead & Pike (2006) I look at values across the curriculum and explore those implicit in different school subjects.

5   Consider the Horn Book or Puritan Primer. See Demers & Moyles (1982).

6   See Pike (2004). In this lecture I reflect that, as a student of English literature throughout grammar school and at University, I was never encouraged to bring my faith to my reading. I believe teaching young readers about the reading process is central to their ability to bring their worldview to the texts they read. With the right approach, young readers can understand transactional theory and notions such as text as 'stimulus' (cf. Pike, 2002a). Since writing this article I have taught transactional theory to children aged 12 but believe it could be taught to much younger children using Venn diagrams (where one circle represents the reader and the other the text and the overlap is the work evoked by the reader). More research is needed on teaching reading as a transaction in Christian contexts. The responses of students at Calvin College are recorded in Smith (2004, p. 144).

7   http://www.christian.org.uk/soregs/sor_booklet_sept06.pdf. The Christian Institute web site provides examples of reading for primary schools in the UK recommended by the Department for Education and Skills. This includes books such as *Daddy's Roommate* by Michael Willhoite, where a father's homosexual relationship is presented as a morally acceptable alternative lifestyle. Given the recently passed Sexual Orientation Legislation in the UK, the possibility exists that such books could be prescribed reading in all schools.

8   "If ye abide in me, and my words abide in you, ye shall *ask what ye will*, and it shall be done unto you" (John 15:7, my italics).

9   Schools often seem to focus more on teaching children to answer other people's questions rather than to ask their own.

10   This book ought to be on the reading list of college-level English education courses.

11   Classic texts such as 'The Latest Decalogue' by Arthur Hugh Clough might be especially valuable for Christian readers. For an example of a teaching sequence with this text see Pike (2003b). Text choice is important, and classical texts should play an important part in a Christian school's reading curriculum.

12   Overman, C. *Assumptions That Affect Our Lives* (Louisiana: Micah Publishing, 1996) and Sampson, P. J., *Six Modern Myths About Christianity and Western Civilization* (Downers Grove: IVP, 2000) are two books on assumptions well worth reading.

13   See Pike (2005b), where I stress the importance of children educated in Christian schools learning to understand and appreciate the views of those with whom they disagree.

14   A number of teaching strategies have been developed to help teachers engage with readers' personal transactions with texts (cf. Pike, 2003c). Annotation, reader response journals and paired dialogue are just some of the methods used to record students' response to text as stimulus. Also see Pike (2004a) for an overview of how to engage with individual readers' transactions. More research is needed in Christian contexts on how Christian readers bring their faith to their reading. A start has been made at Bradford Christian School (cf. Pike, 2005a).

15   Rosenblatt was interested in more than literary theory and was especially concerned with anthropology, human relations and the 'educational needs of a democracy' (Rosenblatt, 1994, p. xiii). Rosenblatt's declared aim was 'to develop a philosophy of literature and teaching that would explain why and under what circumstances the reading of literary works would have both an intrinsic aesthetic value and make possible *the development and assimilation of insights into human relations*' (1994, pp. 179-180; my italics). Rosenblatt was influenced by John Dewey and concludes the revised edition of *The Reader, The Text, The Poem* (1994, p. 188) with Dewey's claim: 'democracy will have its consummation when free social inquiry is wedded to the art of full and moving communication' (Dewey, 1984, p. 350). It was John Dewey who famously observed in *Education and Democracy* that 'democracy is more than a form of government; it is primarily a mode of associated *living*' (Dewey, 1966/2002, p. 101; my italics). I point out in Pike (2007a) that citizenship education seeks to teach children how to *live*. Rosenblatt asserted the aesthetic value of literature and saw this as central to achieving the wide-ranging humanistic aims of education in a democracy (Rosenblatt, 2005, p. xxxiii). It can be dangerous when children are taught to put too much faith in democracy (cf. Pike, 2007b). In the present article I deliberately consider the value of literature in achieving Christian educational aims in a secular, democratic society (cf. also Pike, 2004c).

16   See Tompkins (1980) for an overview.

17   Readers should be encouraged to transact their transactions with each other (cf. Pike, 2003c). One of the ways we can engage in Christian witness is by honestly sharing our Christian perspectives on the texts we read. Far too often, belief is seen as an obstacle to the reading process (cf. Pike, 2003a).

18   On whether schools do teach children to challenge the status quo and welcome competing worldviews, see Pike (2007).

Bibliography

Auden, W. H. (1962). *The dyer's hand and other essays*. London: Faber.

Carr, D. (2004). On the grammar of religious discourse and education. *Zeitschrift für Erziehungswissenschaft*, 7, 380-393.

Demers, P., & Moyles, G. (Eds.). (1982). *From instruction to delight: An anthology of children's literature to 1850*. Oxford: Oxford University Press.

Dewey, J. (1984). The public and its problems. In J. A. Boydston (Ed.), *The later works of John Dewey, 1925-1953: Vol. 2*. Carbondale, IL: Southern Illinois University Press.

Dewey, J. (2002). *Democracy and education*. New York: Macmillan. (Orginal work published 1966)

Eliot, T. S. (1935). Religion and literature. In *Selected essays*. London: Faber & Faber.

Gallagher, S. V., & Lundin, R. (1989). *Literature through the eyes of faith*. San Francisco: HarperCollins.

Hall, K. (2003). *Listening to Stephen read: Multiple perspectives on literacy*. Buckingham: Open University Press.

Halstead, J. M.. & Pike, M. A. (2006). *Citizenship and moral education: Values in action*. London: Routledge.

Hand, M. (2006). Against autonomy as an educational aim. *Oxford Review of Education*, 32, 535-550.

Hilton, M. (2003). Mary Hilton's observations, suggestions and theoretical perspectives. In Hall, K. (Ed.), *Listening to Stephen read*. Buckingham: Open University Press.

Hunt, G. (1989). *Honey for a child's heart: The imaginative use of books in family life*. Grand Rapids, MI: Zondervan.

Ireland, J. (2004). The Christian mind and children's literature. In J. Ireland, R. Edlin, & K. Dickens (Eds.), *Pointing the way: Directions for Christian education in a new millennium* (pp. 55-70). Richmond, NSW, Australia: National Institute for Christian Education.

Iser, W. (1971). Indeterminacy and the reader's response in prose fiction. In Hillis J. Miller (Ed.), *Aspects of narrative*. Columbia, NY: Columbia University Press.

Jacobs, A. (2001). *A theology of reading: The hermeneutics of love*. Boulder, CO: Westview Press.

Jackson, R. (2003). Should the state fund faith based schools? A review of the arguments. *British Journal of Religious Education, 25*, 89-102.

Jauss, H. R. (1982). *Toward an aesthetic of reception* (T. Bahti, Trans.). Minneapolis: Minneapolis University Press. (Original work published 1970)

Lewis, C. S. (1978). *The abolition of man: Reflections on education with special reference to the teaching of English in the upper forms of schools*. Glasgow: Collins/Fount Paperbacks. (Original work published 1943)

Luke, A., Carrington, V., & Kapitzke, C. (2003). Textbooks and early childhood literacy. In J. Marsh (Ed.), *Handbook of early childhood literacy* (pp. 249-257). London: Falmer.

MacIntyre, A. (1988). *Whose justice? Which rationality?* Notre Dame, IN: Notre Dame University Press.

MacIntyre, A. (1990). *Three rival versions of moral enquiry*. Notre Dame, IN: Notre Dame University Press.

McClean, A. (1999, November). What should our children read? *Faith in education*. Durham: The Christian Institute.

Nichols, B. (2000). *Literature in Christian perspective: Becoming faithful readers* London: Darton, Longman, and Todd.

Pike, M. A. (2000a). Keen readers: Adolescents and pre-twentieth century poetry. *Educational Review, 52*, 13-28.

Pike, M. A. (2000b). Spirituality, morality and poetry. *International Journal of Children's Spirituality, 5*, 177-191.

Pike, M. A. (2002a) Pupils' poetics. *Changing English: Studies in reading and culture, 7*, 45-54.

Pike, M. A. (2002b). Aesthetic distance and the spiritual journey: Educating for morally and spiritually significant events across the art and literature curriculum. *International Journal of Children's Spirituality, 7*, 9-21.

Pike, M. A. (2003a). Belief as an obstacle to reading: The case of the Bible? *Journal of Beliefs and Values 24*, 155-163.

Pike, M. A. (2003b). The canon in the classroom: Students' experiences of texts from other times. *Journal of Curriculum Studies, 35*, 355-370.

Pike, M. A. (2003c). From personal to social transaction: A model of aesthetic reading in the classroom. *Journal of Aesthetic Education, 37*, 61-72.

Pike, M. A. (2003d). The Bible and the reader's response. *Journal of Education and Christian Belief, 7*, 37-52.

Pike, M. A. (2004a). *Teaching secondary English*. London: Sage/Paul Chapman Publishing.

Pike, M. A. (2004b). The challenge of Christian schooling in a secular society. *Journal of Research on Christian Education, 13*, 149-166.

Pike, M. A. (2004c, October 19). From personal to spiritual transaction: The potential of aesthetic reading. Kuyers Institute lecture delivered at Calvin College, Michigan, USA. Retrieved June 29, 2007, from http://www.calvin.edu/kuyers/files/Pike041019/Lecture.pdf

Pike, M. A. (2004d). The spiritual gift of reading. *International Journal of Children's Spirituality, 9*, 124-126.

Pike, M. A. (2005a) Reading and responding to biblical texts: Aesthetic distance and the spiritual journey. In C. Ota, & C. Erricker (Eds.), *Spiritual education: Literary, empirical and pedagogical perspectives.* Brighton, UK: Sussex Academic Press.

Pike, M. A. (2005b). Citizenship education and faith schools: What should children in Christian schools understand and appreciate about a liberal and secular society? *Journal of Education and Christian Belief, 9,* 35-46.

Pike, M. A. (2006). From beliefs to skills: The secularization of literacy and the moral education of citizens. *Journal of Beliefs and Values, 27,* 281-289.

Pike, M. A. (2007a, May 9). The state and citizenship education in England: A curriculum for subjects or citizens? *Journal of Curriculum Studies.* Published online May 9, 2007, at http://www.informaworld.com/smpp/title~content=g768140662

Pike, M. A. (2007b). Faith in citizenship: On teaching children to believe in liberal democracy. *British Journal of Religious Education* (forthcoming).

Roques, M. (1989). *Curriculum unmasked: Towards a Christian understanding of education.* Eastbourne: Monarch/Christians in Education, 1989.

Rosenblatt, L. (1968). *Literature as exploration.* London: Heinemann.

Rosenblatt, L. (1985). The transactional theory of the literary work: Implications for research. In C. R. Cooper (Ed.), *Researching response to literature and the teaching of literature: Points of departure.* Norwood, NY: Ablex.

Rosenblatt, L. (1994). *The reader, the text, the poem: The transactional theory of the literary work: With a new preface and epilogue.* Carbondale, IL: Southern Illinois University Press.

Rosenblatt, L. (2005). *Making meaning with texts: Selected essays.* Portsmouth: Heinemann.

Smith, D. (2004). The poet, the child and the blackbird: Aesthetic reading and spiritual development. *International Journal of Children's Spirituality, 9,* 143-144.

Tompkins, J. (Ed.). (1980). *Reader response criticism.* Baltimore: Johns Hopkins University Press.

Wright, A. (2003). Freedom, equality, fraternity? Towards a liberal defence of faith community schools. *British Journal of Religious Education, 25,* 142-152.

JE&CB 11:2 (2007) 95-107   1366-5456

Cynthia G. Slagter
Approaching Interpretive Virtues Through Reading Aloud

EDUCATORS ARE OFTEN frustrated when students appear not to have completed reading assignments carefully or attentively and seem unwilling or unable to give a fair and balanced critique of what they have read. This essay suggests that incorporating the practice of reading aloud may help both to point out where students are stumbling and to create an environment in which they can learn to pay close, careful, just attention to a text.

It was a hot afternoon, and my fellow eighth-grade students and I were restless and irritable. And now our teacher was planning to read aloud to us from a collection of Edgar Alan Poe short stories. We were not interested in a long-dead nineteenth-century author, and we were certainly far too old to be read to! Nonetheless, as the teacher began to read "The Tell-Tale Heart," we were steadily drawn in to the rhythms of the language and began paying attention to the story. Slowly, deliberately, the teacher began to drum his foot against the desk, mimicking the steady, inexorable heartbeat of the victim in the story, the volume of his drumming increasing with the paranoia of the narrator. Our rapt attention was shattered when, as the tale came to its dramatic conclusion, the teacher shrieked along with the narrator: "I admit the deed! – tear up the planks! here, here! – It is the beating of his hideous heart!"

Even though this incident occurred decades ago, I have never forgotten it and actually think about it rather often. Did my teacher do justice to the text as he read? I believe so. He took the black marks on the white page and transformed them into a visceral, unforgettable experience. Hearing the text read aloud helped us to overcome the barrier of the unfamiliar syntax, to understand words in context. It transported us from a poor, rural community to a sophisticated, urban setting. We were pulled out of ourselves to experience, in a small way, what it might be like to be in another's skin. His reading modeled for us what it meant to interact with a text, to allow a text to move from being something external and alien to being internalized and influential. Due partly to the impact of those words on that hot summer day, I have incorporated reading aloud into my own classes. Not only do I read to my students, I also require them to read aloud to themselves and to others. While hearing a text read aloud provides access to one person's interpretation and can kindle a delight in reading and literature, reading a text aloud requires the reader to examine the text carefully, to pay close attention, to make choices, and to deal honestly with the words on the page. Only then can a reader attempt to render those words faithfully for an audience. The resulting vocal performance provides evidence of this process: "Reading is vocal interpretation. When we read in public, our own personal understanding of and emotional reaction to what we read comes out in our manner of reading" (Smit, 1996). Reading aloud, when practiced regularly and respectfully, can help students to grapple with reading justly and charitably by teaching them to approach a text humbly, to read and reread a text until it begins to give up its meaning, and to be willing to empty themselves and take on, temporarily, the voice of another. Using oral reading to connect to an aural comprehension, both the listeners' and the readers' understanding, appreciation, and enjoyment of a text are enhanced. What could be a relatively passive, solitary experience – silent, solo reading – becomes communal and active.

Teaching Virtues in the Academy

When considering incorporating the virtues into the classroom, it is perhaps common to think of exhorting students to "love their neighbor as themselves" or to "do justice" in the sense of social activism. While it is certainly the responsibility of Christians to teach love of neighbor and to foster justice in social and political spheres, the Christian academic also has the responsibility to foster justice and charity in the habits of the mind. On this theme, I was especially struck by the words of Mark Schwehn (1993) in his book *Exiles from Eden*. Discussing criticism regarding his study of William James, both self-criticism and criticism from others, he says that he stands accused of not being *charitable* to James, or of not doing him *justice*. Schwehn remarks, "Notice that the vocabulary of moral and spiritual value – here justice and charity – easily insinuates itself into appraisals of thought as well as action" (p. 50). Schwehn compares our attitudes toward living human beings and texts: just as our efforts to treat people justly and charitably require empathy and openness, so too cultivating an attitude of charity and justice toward a text requires a sympathetic approach, "more cautious in appraisal, ... less prone to stereotype and caricature" (p. 51). A calling to justice and charity is just as relevant and just as urgent inside our classrooms, where we cultivate the habits of the mind, as in our larger communities, where we may be more concerned with matters of social justice. After all, justice is more than an aim of political activity, and charity is more than a pleasant disposition. They are attributes of God that should characterize all aspects of human activity in every realm of life. Although a large proportion of academic life is spent interacting with texts, both fictional and non-fictional, little attention is paid to the idea of helping students apply the concepts of justice and charity to their reading.

My particular field is Spanish literature, but much of what follows is relevant to any text-based course. In my discipline, students are regularly made aware of the need for them to *do* justice – to love the alien, to bring shalom – but their conception of these virtues is often limited to the idea that justice and charity are gifts or blessings that they have received and that they must bestow upon others. More difficult for them than the notion of active, muscular "doing justice" in a social setting is the idea of *being* just, that is, being fair, humble, and charitable when confronting an Other. Micah 6:8 links justice with humility and kindness, and in our classrooms we too must guide students to read texts and confront the Other found in those texts with an attitude of justice, charity, and humility. After all, Christians acknowledge the Other as never entirely other, recognizing that we are all image-bearers of God.

But what does it mean to read justly and charitably? Just as "justice" can be a slippery term in a socio-political context, it can also cause problems in the arena of literary interpretation. Perhaps it is easier to define what it is not. Reading justly does not mean finding the interpretation that best fits the assigning professor's worldview. Reading justly does not mean forcing a Christian interpretation on a non-Christian text. Reading justly does not mean dismissing a text as too hard, or too dull, or too dense after a cursory reading. It does mean being receptive to a text, being open to see what the text can offer to the reader. Reading justly also means recognizing what the text says even if the reader does not agree. Reading justly presupposes engaging with a text again and again, struggling with it in an attempt to understand. With that in mind, consider the challenges instructors face when attempting to help students engage justly, humbly, and kindly with a text. There are many. Students may have convinced themselves that a text is too difficult and therefore not worth their time. They may give only cursory attention to a text before passing (an often harsh) judgment. Or they may simply say no, refusing to open themselves to a viewpoint or an idea alien or frightening to them.

Alan Jacobs (2001), in his book *A Theology of Reading: The Hermeneutics of Love*, refers again and again to the need for "charitable readers," readers who "offer the gift of constant and loving attention – faithfulness – to a story, a poem, to an argument, in hope that it will be rewarded" (p. 89). Both secular and Christian scholars agree that, as Robert Scholes (2002) asserts,

> a good person, in our time, needs to have the rhetorical capacity to imagine the other's thought, feeling, and sentiments .... It is our responsibility as ... teachers to help our students develop this form of textual power, in which strength comes, paradoxically, from subordinating one's own thoughts temporarily to the views and values of another person. (p. 168)

Jacobs puts this in explicitly Christian terms:

> Genuine love of others is kenotic in a particular sense of the word: Genuine love of others requires an emptying out of one's own self and a consequent refilling of the emptied consciousness with attention to the Other. (p. 104)

The task, then, is to move students from being resistant readers to being kenotic readers. Both Schwehn and Jacobs have offered compelling arguments for the need for reading justly and charitably, but neither offers much in the way of concrete praxis. I believe that one way to approach just and charitable reading is through reading aloud. Reading aloud is an invitation to students to temporarily shed their own opinions and prejudices and to take on the mind of the Other.

Considering the challenges

Unfortunately, the first challenge that we face in teaching students to read justly may arise because our culture often downgrades reading, an attitude students may absorb. A colleague related to me that he once had a student scornfully ask why we paid so much attention to reading; it's only literature after all, and not life.[1] My students often seem to come with a preconceived notion of text. Indeed, in this age dominated by visual rather than verbal imagery, they increasingly regard literary and academic texts in general as mysterious and somewhat impenetrable. This may be why they fail to read beyond difficult vocabulary and complex sentence structure to discover what the author is trying to express. Some students, after briefly struggling with a reading, will declare that it is too hard, too vague, not relevant, or simply "no good." Schwehn narrates just such an incident when he had assigned a passage from St. Augustine. He was surprised and distressed when, after a quick reading, students dismissed the passage in a peremptory way, complaining that it was "unnecessarily obscure" (p. 48).

Second, in classes that require significant reading – be it literary or non-literary – students may report having dutifully completed their homework, yet it may become clear that they have failed to read with care and are left with only a superficial knowledge of the text. Not surprisingly, many students, pressed for time and pressured to complete many assignments, fail to read slowly and carefully. Perhaps they are able to answer the "who, what, why, where" questions, but they have neglected to understand the work in its context or to notice its artistic qualities. Although they ostensibly *have* read the material, they may not have perceived the work's tone or detected the author's slant and therefore may be prone to unjust or uncharitable interpretations. Sadly, I have to include myself in this group. As a very rapid reader, all too often I have failed to appreciate an author's lovely phrasing or have missed a stunning image. For me, it was reading in a second language, a process that forced me to slow down and savor what I read, that reawakened a delight in reading and interpreting text.[2] While we want students to acquire the ability to skim and scan texts, sometimes it seems that they – like I – have learned this lesson too well: they have forgotten how to linger over a text, how to read and reread until the text gives up its meaning. Much of the academy seems to train students to read in what Louise Rosenblatt (1978) calls an "efferent" way, that is, to read for information only.[3] Students approach the text attempting to "get out of it" the necessary information in the most efficient way possible, but fail to linger to enjoy or appreciate its artistic aspects or to understand satirical or ironic undertones.

Finally, some students may be resistant readers, reading in what Arlene Wilner (2002) calls "such willfully naïve ways that, instead of interpreting or even shedding light on the text, they [appear] simply to deny it" (p. 173). Such students resist moving beyond the world of their own experience, seeking only those reading experiences which reaffirm and reinforce world and life views that mirror and agree with their own. Upper-middle class students, unable or unwilling to identify with an uneducated or poor character in a text may fail to recognize an author's condemnation of certain social practices. They may not realize that some statements are meant ironically, not literally. Christian students may view all texts through a biblical lens, leading to some strange interpretations and suspect theology.[4]

How Reading Aloud May Help

Of course, part of the problem in identifying poor reading practices is that most reading is an invisible process. As Robert Scholes (2002) declares, "We do not see reading. We see some writing about reading, to be sure, but we do not see reading." (p. 166). Perhaps something has been lost in our great advance from an oral to a print culture. As Walter Ong (1977) recognizes,

> The fecundity of the text … is realizable only through its connection with the oral world. In this sense, text as text is essentially dead. For texts are there to produce words, which are irreducibly sounds, realized orally either in the externalized utterance or in the internalized imagination. (p. 258)

Because of this, one possible tool to help our students become better, more charitable, and just readers is reading aloud. Restoring the oral/aural element to literature can provide a new dimension from which students can learn. Scholes asserts: "Reading aloud makes the reading process evident to the ear in tone and rhythm and to the eye in bodily posture and facial expression, just as writing makes the composition process evident in written signs" (p. 168). But how can reading aloud address each of the barriers to just and charitable reading mentioned above?

I return to Schwehn and the incident of his students' reaction to St. Augustine. He declares that "much of what passes for laziness or the proverbial 'lack of motivation' among today's students really involves a lack of humility, stemming in part from a lack of piety or respect for that aspect of God's ongoing creation that manifests itself in works of genius" (p. 48). While he goes on to mention various ways in which he might have failed to properly present the text, he also declares, "My students could have overcome my failings had they been sufficiently humble; had they presumed that Augustine's apparent obscurity was their problem, not his …. Humility, on this account … means … the presumption of wisdom and authority in the author" (p. 48). Hopefully, Schwehn's students were persuaded to go back to the text and try again to discover what Augustine was saying.

Like Schwehn's students and their reaction to St. Augustine, some of my students are initially dismissive of Miguel de Unamuno, an author of the Spanish "Generation of '98" who writes with an obvious philosophical bent. Although his novel, San Manuel Bueno, mártir, is one of his most straightforward texts, students appear to lack the patience to decipher the more complex sentences. Near the end of the novel, the narrator makes a pivotal statement about the main character's faith, yet when asked about it, many students admitted that they had not taken the time to try to understand it, "knowing" that it would be too difficult. Rather than curiosity or a desire to understand what the author might be trying to say, they expressed frustration and then simply passed over the text. They lacked the patience, and perhaps the necessary humility, to overcome the apparent obscurity of the text with careful and repeated readings.

The passage in question reads:

Creo que Don Manuel Bueno, que mi san Manuel y que mi hermano

Lázaro se murieron creyendo no creer lo que más nos interesa, pero sin creer creerlo, creyéndolo en una desolación activa y resignada. (1930/1988, p. 146)

(I believe that Don Manuel the Good, that my Saint Manuel, and that my brother Lazarus died believing they did not believe in what most interests us, but without believing they believed it, were believing it in an active and resigned desolation. [My translation])

It is true; this passage is difficult and bewildering at first. The author has structured the sentence so that it *will* be difficult to read, so that the reader will slow down and notice what is being said. Here reading aloud – reading the punctuation and reading the various grammatical permutations of the verb *creer* "to believe" – can help students to open themselves up to understand what Unamuno is saying. In class I require that students read the text aloud first to themselves and then to a partner once, twice, three times, constantly discussing what it means and how it can best be read aloud to express and reveal its meaning. Reading and rereading aloud helps students to untangle complex syntax and eventually arrive at an understanding of the meaning of the passage. Slowly students recognize the power and subtlety of Unamuno's language. Finally, they model their readings for the class, and together the class discusses the implications of the various emphases. This prolonged and humble contact with the text has helped students do interpretive justice to the complicated and paradoxical beliefs of Miguel de Unamuno.

Unfortunately, we are often disappointed when we ask students to read aloud. Jerome McGann notes:

Over some years I have observed the (perhaps increasing) disability that students have in negotiating language in an articulate way. This weakness seems to propagate others, most especially an inclination to 'read' texts at relatively high levels of textual abstraction. With diminished skills in perceiving words as such comes, it seems, a weakened ability to notice other close details of language – semantic, grammatical, rhetorical. Recitation – I am talking about oral recitation of the fictional text – forces students to return to elementary levels of linguistic attention. To be effective as a pedagogical tool, however, it must be performed regularly and explicitly discussed and reflected upon. These exercises form the basis for developing higher-level acts of linguistic attention. (p. 147)

What McGann mentions here as a disability is, of course, closely related to Rosenblatt's notion of efferent reading. Students skim over the surface of a reading, picking out what they believe to be the relevant "facts" without taking time to delve into the deeper, richer levels. As McGann recognizes, however, oral recitation must be practiced, analyzed, and critiqued for it to be truly helpful.

In my advanced Spanish literature courses, one of the authors we study is Mariano José de Larra, a nineteenth-century Spanish author. His works are bitingly satirical and offer a sharp criticism of the customs of the Spanish middle class, but like so many works of the nineteenth century they are dense, full of complex sentences, many with ironic undertones. Perhaps not surprisingly, the students' initial reaction to him is fairly negative. Unlike the easily comprehended, ribald humor of Cervantes, Larra's sense of humor requires that students dedicate time and energy to a careful reading of the nuances of the text. In an attempt to help students recognize the satirical tone of Larra's writing, I ask them to read certain passages aloud. Like McGann, I am often initially disappointed. Whereas during the Middle Ages "the persistent habit of reading aloud, and the preference, even among the educated, for listening to a statement rather than scrutinizing it in script, comprised popular literary practices" (Glenn, 1993, p. 498), modern-day students are unpracticed and therefore less than effective in their first attempt. A revival of medieval practices of reading aloud in community helps students overcome their initial resistance to a difficult passage. The exercise of reading aloud, discussing in a group, and reflecting on the accuracy and effectiveness of an interpretation facilitate deeper understanding and a greater appreciation for a text. The students' encounter with Larra illustrates this.

The Larra text, "El castellano viejo," involves the account of an uncomfortable evening spent dining at the home of a loud-mouthed buffoon, with the narrator's ironic commentary on all present. As such it lends itself to group work, with students taking roles of various characters and reading specific sections of the text aloud in such a way that the meaning of the text can be revealed through their interpretation. Studying the text in this way moves reading from an individual, isolated task to a community endeavor. As the students practice their sections aloud, together they decide the meaning and significance of certain phrases and determine the best way to communicate these meanings orally. Slowly the students become aware of the tone of their passages and recognize the humorous implications of the story. Their final oral interpretation normally illustrates a clear understanding of the nuances of the text. Through this experience they learn that, when read and reread patiently, many a text will give up its secrets and reward the reader with a deeper understanding. By approaching the text charitably, taking the time to allow the text to speak to them across the centuries, the students move beyond their early, swift dismissal of Larra and his relevance to a fuller, more just interpretation of text and its author.

Reading Aloud to Foster Empathy

Finally, I return to the problem of resistant readers. Our students are sometimes hindered from relating to others by their identification with their own socioeconomic circumstances. They appear willfully to ignore an author's message if that message runs counter to what they expect to be true. A case in point is a student interpretation of Ana María Matute's short story "Pecado de omisión" ("Sin of omission"). In the story, thirteen-year-old Lope is entrusted to his wealthy uncle's care after his mother dies. Against the local teacher's advice the uncle decides not to allow Lope to attend school but instead sends him to the mountains to tend sheep. The boy remains there in isolation for years, visited occasionally by servants who bring him basic supplies. When he finally returns to the town, he runs into a former classmate who is now studying to be a lawyer. As Lope shakes the other boy's hand he realizes that, compared with the other young man he, Lope, is little more than an animal. In a blind rage, he enters the uncle's home with a large rock and bashes in his skull. As he is led away in handcuffs, the women of the household wail that Lope has killed his benefactor, the one to whom he owes everything he has and is. Lope merely affirms this, crying, "Yes, yes, yes." Responding to a question on the significance of the title, one student enumerated all the instances in which Lope had committed the sin of ingratitude. She determined that Lope's failure to thank his uncle was the sin of omission mentioned in the title. Since this student was a native speaker of Spanish, linguistic barriers could not account for this surprising interpretation. Parker Palmer (1983, 1993) has commented on the tendency of learners to resist things that challenge their preconceived notions of how the world should be because, as he remarks, "we want to know in ways that allow us to convert the world – but we do not want to be known in ways that require us to change as well" (p. 40). This student was unable to put herself into the position of someone so foreign to her own experience. She immediately identified with the wealthy uncle, to the giver of charity and not to the recipient. Her silent, independent reading also did not afford her any corrective analysis that might have caused her to reconsider.

Since the reading of the student mentioned above was silent and individual, it is difficult to know how she arrived at her interpretation. Had this student been asked to read the story aloud as if she were narrating her own, first-person story, perhaps she would have been able to put herself in the place of the young man of the tale. Perhaps if she had worked on an oral interpretation of this text with other students, the group interaction would have led her to see her bias and to interpret the text in another way. Don Geiger (1953), advocating for oral interpretation as an essential element of the literature class, notes that a just interpretation of a passage requires this alignment between text and reader. Describing an effective oral reading, he says, "What is demanded is, roughly, that the attitudes and actions of the reading be congruent with the attitudes and actions of the piece, and in different pieces these attitudes and actions will develop in vastly differently tempos" (p. 283). Achieving this congruence of reader and text is not easy; it requires an openness on the part of the reader, a willingness to learn and explore, and a great deal of patience.

Practicing Reading Aloud

Reading aloud can rarely be done well on the spur of the moment. Students must first be equipped with background information, sufficient preparation time, and knowledge of the audience. Before students begin to interact with a passage, they must understand the context of the work. Knowing about the time and place in which a work was written, as well as something about the author, can help students arrive at a truer interpretation. Time is another important factor; students must be given sufficient time, either in class or outside of class, to experiment with different readings. And perhaps the most important element in this type of performance assignment is to make students aware of their audience. I advise my students that they should consider that their audience is made up of people from the culture and time to which the work was originally directed, and that one member of this audience is the author him- or herself.[5] While they are encouraged to be creative and imaginative in their interpretations, they are reminded to remember always to be fair to the author. If their reading would offend or insult a member of their audience, that reading should be reconsidered.

Cuban author Nicolás Guillén's poem "Sensemayá" reproduces a ritualistic chant, "for killing a snake," filled with nonsense words and ceremonial repetitions. The poem is at first daunting and somewhat intimidating to students, and certainly very foreign to their own life experiences, yet after they have worked to present an oral interpretation of it, they will have learned a great deal, both about the author and the text and about their own beliefs. Before studying the poem itself, we discuss traditions and beliefs in Cuba, santería – the Afro-Caribbean religion that combines beliefs of the Yoruba of West Africa with Roman Catholicism – and issues of religious syncretism. Then students form groups to practice their reading of the poem. They are reminded to remain true to the words and spirit of the author and to the context of the poem. That is, they are to "become" the Other. Ong (1958) has perhaps expressed it best:

> Every human word implies not only the existence – at least in the imagination – of another to whom the word is uttered, but it also implies that the speaker has a kind of otherness within himself. He participates in the other to whom he speaks, and it is this underlying participation that makes communication possible. The human speaker can speak to the other precisely because he himself is not purely self, but is somehow also other." (p. 46)

In general, students genuinely enjoy performing written texts. In the case of the Guillén poem, they have used multiple voicing and choral repetitions, adopting syncopated rhythms to capture the sense of wild abandon. Their interpretations demonstrate a clear understanding of the connections between text and context. They appear to have been successful in emptying out their own American selves and taking on the Caribbean other. Each time I have used oral interpretation as a means to approach a text, I have been impressed with students' creativity and their insights. (A pleasant side-effect has been students' appreciation and respect for one another's work.)

But is this really doing justice to a text? A close reading of Jacobs (and his reading of Mikhail Bakhtin) will reveal that this is not all he means by a kenotic reading. As he warns, often "authors, teachers, … and readers alike engage in a simple hermeneutical system in which the word produced is authoritative and its reception is purely passive. [This] humility is a false humility" (p. 107). Jacobs and Bakhtin warn that the reader must not merely be a blank slate or an empty vessel upon which the author and text can act. Instead, the reader's relationship with the text must be *inter*active, not *re*active. As the students read, react, critique, and revise their interpretations, they are entering into a dialogic relationship with the text, truly experiencing it from within and from without. However, if our students have been able to take on the voice of the Other but have not been moved to respond, to move forward, they not yet truly read the text in a just and charitable way. Once we have carefully, charitably, empathetically read the Other, we are called to respond. A kenotic reading, a just reading, a charitable reading, demands not only interaction but also response.

In classes at my institution, Calvin College, questions of worldview are frequently discussed. With regard to the poem, these might be "What is the spirit of the Guillén poem? Where does it come from? How does it speak to the world? How can/should we react to this as Christians?" Our oral interpretation has revealed the poem as a thing of great aesthetic beauty, but now we must begin what Jacobs sees as "an opposite movement: a distancing, a distinguishing of the other from oneself so that the productive outsidedness can be achieved" (p. 119). In the case of the Guillén poem, our grounding in Scripture tells us that the poem's spiritual foundations are suspect and that we cannot accept wholeheartedly the message that it sends us. Although the snake imagery brings to mind biblical interpretations, students must consider these images within the cultural context of the poem. With each text we are called to help our students shun a naive acceptance of everything an author says while similarly avoiding an unjustly intolerant reading.

The final step in this reading assignment calls for students to apply what they have learned through their empathetic, kenotic oral interpretation of the text and to combine that with their understanding of their faith. The key is not to shift from one mode of interpretation to another, but rather to allow each reading to inform the other so that the final result is a careful, considered, charitable and just reading of the text. To help students do this, the writing assignment that follows this reading is structured in the form of a letter (a technique I've appropriated from Susan Handelman, 2002, and modified somewhat) addressed to the author. While they are encouraged to express concerns and critiques of the work they have read, they must always keep in mind that they are writing to the person who authored this text, the one who invested time and creative energy into its production. This process makes explicit the bidirectional nature of reading. Parker Palmer addresses this same issue, although he talks of truth rather than justice: "Truth involves entering into a relationship with someone or something genuinely other than us, but with whom we are intimately bound" (p. 31), and "Truth requires the knower to become interdependent with the known. Both parties have their own integrity and otherness, and one party cannot be collapsed into the other" (p. 32). Parker here expresses in another way the ideas of Bakhtin: the relationship between reader and text is dialogic; there must be interaction, revelation, and response between text and reader.

Conclusion

As Jacobs, Schwehn, and others have noted, Christians are called to apply the virtues of charity and justice not just to our relationships with people but also to our scholarly activity. As Christian academics we have a further duty to help our students recognize and put into practice this mandate. In an age dominated by the desire for speed and efficiency, we must teach them to linger and to savor a text.

When hubris or laziness causes them to dismiss a text unjustly, we must encourage humility and loving attention. Carefully structured read-aloud assignments can help students to approach texts differently. As marks on a page are transformed into spoken words, the reader's relationship with a text changes. A slower, more intimate connection is possible and therefore the opportunity for understanding and appreciation is created.

Reading aloud will not instantly make difficult texts easy, nor will students suddenly appreciate previously scorned works. Still, the practice of reading aloud can open new avenues of exploration and interpretation of text by encouraging multiple readings of a passage, thereby increasing the possibility of understanding and discerning the author's message. By slowing down the process, reading a text aloud can draw attention to nuances, to inferences, to previously hidden undertones and in so doing enable previously hidden ideas to bubble through. Physically speaking the words, in a sense "owning" them for a time, may help students to put themselves figuratively in another's shoes and to get a better understanding of what an author thinks and feels and believes. In short, reading aloud may help students (and teachers) to read more justly and more charitably.

This is still for me a work in progress, but the results so far have been encouraging. Students are taking time and care with their readings and are being rewarded with increased understanding and an enhanced appreciation of texts. Perhaps someday they too will read a story aloud to another group of students and have the same effect on them that my eighth-grade teacher had on me!

Notes

1   Alas, this attitude appears to be far from unusual; Bárbara Mujica narrates a very similar episode in her preface to the Spanish literary anthology *Texto y vida* (p.iii).

2   Interestingly, it is adversity that helps to bring an appreciation of text. A colleague shared with me the following story, heard on the program *Fresh Air*: "It should be said that I am not severely dyslexic, I am mildly dyslexic. I think from the time I was a kid and slow to learn to read in the first and second grades and third grades that I had to learn to read very slowly, much more slowly than was true for my classmates in Mississippi in the 40s, ah 50s rather and that one of the things I fell heir to were all of those so to say poetical aspects of language, the non-specifically cognitive aspects (in which language is just a vehicle for communication), so that I became quite aware in my mouth and in my ear of language's sonorities and its syncopations and rhythms and pauses and meter and all of those things about prose indeed and that in fact that enhanced my appreciation of language and enhanced my appreciation of written literature so that no, it was not at all, other than to slow me down considerably, it was not at all a detriment in causing me to appreciate reading or to be inclined to write … it was me making, I think instinctually, a virtue out of a vice, but goodness gracious there was a virtue there." (Ford, 2006)

3   In *The Reader, the Text, the Poem*, Rosenblatt delineates two opposing ways of reading text: efferently or aesthetically. To read aesthetically requires that the reader engage with the text and bring to it her own life experiences, while an efferent reading seeks only to take away facts or information.

4   See David Smith's article in this volume for an example of an interesting misuse of scriptural analogy.

5   In order to elicit different interpretations, students could be directed to prepare their performance with a number of different audiences in mind. How, for instance, would the poem be performed differently for an audience of believers or non-believers? Or for Cubans versus Spaniards? Claire Kramsch explores ways to use readers' theater to examine various layers of interpretation of text in *Context and Culture in Language Teaching*, especially chapter 3.

Bibliography

Ford, R. (2006, October 26). A conversation with novelist Richard Ford. *Fresh air with Terry Gross* [Radio broadcast]. Retrieved November 3, 2006, from http://www.npr. org/templates/story/story.php?storyId=6387732

Geiger, D. (1953). New perspectives in oral interpretation. *College English*, 14, 281-286.

Glenn, C. (1993). Medieval literacy outside the academy: Popular practice and individual technique. *College Composition and Communication, 44*, 497-508.

Handelman, S. (2002). "Stopping the heart": The spiritual search of students and the challenge to a professor in an undergraduate literature class. In Andrea Sterk (Ed.), *Religion, scholarship, and higher education.* (pp. 202-229). Notre Dame, IN: University of Notre Dame Press.

Jacobs, A. (2001). *A theology of reading: The hermeneutics of love.* Cambridge, MA: Westview Press.

Kramsch, C. (1993). *Context and culture in language teaching.* Oxford: Oxford University Press.

McGann, J. (2001). Reading fiction/Teaching fiction: A pedagogical experiment. *Pedagogy, 1*(1), 143-165.

Mujica, B. (1990). *Texto y vida: Introducción a la literatura española.* Fort Worth, TX: Holt, Rinehart and Winston.

Ong, W. (1958). Voice as a summons for belief: Literature, faith, and the divided self. *Thought: A Review of Culture and Idea, 33*, 43-61.

Ong, W. (1977). *Interfaces of the word: Studies in the evolution of consciousness and culture.* Ithaca and London: Cornell University Press.

Ong, W. (1978). Literacy and orality in our times. *ADE Bulletin, 58*, 1-7.

Palmer, P. (1983, 1993). *To know as we are known.* San Francisco: Harper Collins.

Rosenblatt, L. M. (1978). *The reader, the text, the poem.* Carbondale and Edwardsville, IL: Southern Illinois University Press.

Scholes, R. (2002). The transition to college reading. *Pedagogy, 2*, 165-172.

Schwehn, M. R. (1993). *Exiles from Eden: Religion and the academic vocation in America.* Oxford: Oxford University Press.

Smit, H. (1996). *So you've been asked to ... read Scripture.* [Brochure]. Grand Rapids: CRC Publications.

Wilner, A. (2002). Confronting resistance: Sonny's blues – and mine. *Pedagogy, 2*, 173-196.

Unamuno, M. de. (1988). *San Manuel Bueno, mártir.* Madrid: Ediciones Cátedra. (Original work published 1930)

Appendix

Writing Assignment: "Sensemaya" Nicolás Guillén

Choose one of the following options. Your paper should be ca. 500 words in length.

A. Write a letter to Nicolás Guillén in which you express your appreciation for the poem. Tell him what you enjoyed about it and why. This is also your opportunity to ask for more information. Were there elements of the poem that you did not understand? concepts that confused or concerned you? State what those were and explain your questions in as much detail as possible. Explain briefly your own belief system and what impact that has had on your reading of the poem.

B. Write a letter to Nicolás Guillén describing your group's interpretative reading of his poem. State what you did and why you did it that way. Explain how you incorporated your own beliefs/faith into your interpretation of the poem. Mention any discussions or conflicts that occurred within the group as you were preparing your reading. Include an evaluation of your performance and any questions or clarifications that you would like the author to provide.

C. Write a letter to one of the other groups who performed a reading of the poem. Express your reaction to their reading. What elements surprised you most? What did you appreciate most? What led you to a better/different interpretation of the poem than what you had before? Are there aspects of their reading that you disagree with? Why? How would you have handled those elements? Did anything in the reading reveal to you the beliefs/attitude of the group? What and how?

D. Write a lesson plan for a high school teacher using this reading exercise. Explain why and how it can be a useful tool for interpretation. List any cautions or reservations you may have. Outline in detail all of the steps in the process.

Journal of Education & Christian Belief

Concerned with current educational thinking from a Christian perspective

EDITORS:
Dr. John Shortt
Dr. David I. Smith
Dr. John Sullivan

MANAGEMENT GROUP:
Ben Jones (The Stapleford Centre)
Rupert Kaye (Association of Christian Teachers)
Dr. Andrew Marfleet
Dr. John Shortt
Dr. David I. Smith (The Kuyers Institute)
Dr. John Sullivan

EDITORIAL ADVISERS:
Professor Harro Van Brummelen, Trinity Western University, Canada.
Dr. Allan Harkness, Asia Graduate School of Theology, Singapore.
Dr. Susan Hasseler, Calvin College, USA.
Professor Brian V. Hill, Murdoch University, Australia.
Rev. Dr. William K. Kay, University of Wales, Wales.
Dr. D. Barry Lumsden, University of Alabama, USA.
Samson Makhado, Association of Christian Schools International, South Africa.
Dr. Mark Pike, University of Leeds, England.
Dr. Signe Sandsmark, Norwegian Lutheran Mission, Norway.
Dr. Pablo J. Santana Bonilla, University of La Laguna, Tenerife, Spain.
Dr. Elmer J. Thiessen, Medicine Hat College, Canada.
Professor Michael S. Totterdell, Manchester Metropolitan University, England.
Professor Keith Watson, University of Reading, England.

SPONSORING BODIES:

Association of Christian Teachers, 94A London Road, St. Albans, AL1 1NX, England. (www.christian-teachers.org.uk)
Kuyers Institute for Christian Teaching and Learning, Calvin College, 3201 Burton St SE, Grand Rapids MI 49546, USA. (www.pedagogy.net)
The Stapleford Centre, The Old Lace Mill, Frederick Road, Stapleford, Nottingham, NG9 8FN, England. (www.stapleford-centre.org)

INDEXING:

This journal is indexed in the British Education Index, Religion Index One: Periodicals (RIO), Religious & Theological Abstracts, Research into Higher Education Abstracts, Educational Research Abstracts Online and a number of other abstracting and indexing sources.

Typeset by Toucan Design, Exeter, England and printed in the USA for The Stapleford Centre by Color House Graphics, Grand Rapids, MI.

Current Subscription Rates						
Period	Institutions			Individuals		
	UK	USA and Canada	Elsewhere Overseas	UK	USA and Canada	Elsewhere Overseas
One Year	£24.10	62.75 USD	£25.10	£24.10	41.40 USD	£25.10
Two/Three Years, Per Year	£22.10	56.50 USD	£22.60	£22.10	37.30 USD	£22.60

2/3rds world, individuals and institutions:
50% discount on the overseas sterling (£) rates listed above
All subscriptions to:
The Stapleford Centre, The Old Lace Mill, Frederick Road, Stapleford, Nottingham
NG9 8FN, UK
Tel: +44 (0) 115 939 6270; Fax: +44 (0) 115 939 2076; Email: subs@jecb.org
Secure online payment of subscriptions by credit card is available at www.jecb.org.

ISSN: 1366-5456
ISBN: 978-1-902234-65-5

Instructions to Contributors

EDITORIAL ADDRESSES:

USA and Canada:

Dr. David Smith, JE&CB Editor,
The Kuyers Institute, Calvin College, 3201 Burton Street SE, Grand Rapids,
Michigan 49546, USA. Email: jecb@calvin.edu.

Dr. Jan Simonson, JE&CB Reviews Editor,
Education Department, Calvin College, 3201 Burton Street SE, Grand Rapids,
Michigan 49546, USA. Email: jecb@calvin.edu.

UK and Rest of World:

Dr. John Shortt, JE&CB Editor,
1 Kiteleys Green, Leighton Buzzard, Beds., LU7 3LD, UK.
Email: editor@jecb.org.

Dr. John Sullivan, JE&CB Editor,
Arts & Humanities Deanery, Liverpool Hope University, Hope Park, Liverpool
L16 9JD, UK. Email: sullivj@hope.ac.uk.

Dr. Peter Shepherd, JE&CB Reviews Editor,
Homestead, Eastham St., Clitheroe, Lancashire BB7 2HY, UK.
Email: reviews@jecb.org

ARTICLES:
Manuscripts for publication and other editorial correspondence should be addressed to one of the Editors at the appropriate address above.

Manuscripts of 4,000 to 5,000 words should be submitted as a file in a standard word-processing format to the appropriate editorial emailing address. Everything, including notes, should be double-spaced. To facilitate anonymous review by referees, the author's name should not appear in the article. Please include, however, a separate cover sheet that should contain: the article title, an abstract of up to 100 words, the author's name and full contact details, a single sentence professional self-description, up to six key words and phrases that describe the article's focus, and a statement that the article is original and has not been published elsewhere. Contributors should retain copies of their files since the Editors can take no responsibility in case of loss or damage. Acceptance of manuscripts is subject to the journal's peer review policy (see www.jecb.org). Authors should bear in mind that they are addressing an international readership and avoid or explain local jargon.

References: Text and citations should conform to the *Publication Manual of the American Psychological Association* (5th edition). A full bibliography of works cited should appear at the end of the article. Endnotes should be numbered consecutively in the text

BOOK REVIEWS:

Books for review should be sent to either Dr. Jan Simonson (USA and Canada) or Dr. Peter Shepherd (UK and Rest of World) at the addresses on the previous page.

Full instructions to reviewers will be sent together with books for review.

Suggestions are welcome from readers regarding books which they consider should be reviewed in the journal.

NOTES & NEWS:

Items for our Notes & News section should be sent to the Editors. Details of publications and major conferences of interest to our readers are particularly welcome.

COPYRIGHT:

Copyright for all articles and book reviews will be retained by the Association of Christian Teachers, The Kuyers Institute for Christian Teaching and Learning, and The Stapleford Centre.

If authors or book reviewers wish to re-publish all or part of their contributions elsewhere, permission should be gained from the Editors and mention of its first publication in the *Journal of Education and Christian Belief* should be made.

Single copies of articles and book reviews may be made for research and/or private study without permission. Permission to make multiple copies in the UK must be obtained from the Copyright Licensing Agency Ltd, 90 Tottenham Court Road, London W1P 9HE. Permission to make multiple copies in the rest of the world must be sought via the publishers.